May We Learn from the Earth

Nature Poems and Reflections on the Environment

by

Robert J. Tiess

Dedication

for
Sandra,

my world

Welcome

Welcome, friend. I'm deeply grateful for this opportunity to offer my words and thoughts for your consideration.

With the wellness of Earth and the wonders of existence in mind, I have attempted to create an ambitious yet accessible book that could be engaged and appreciated by many different readers, from budding poetry lovers to future nature enthusiasts, environmental advocates, and others. Everyone is welcome and respected here.

Poems in the following pages reflect on nature from a variety of perspectives. I'm always amazed and inspired by our beautiful planet and the natural realm. In any direction, at any distance, something awaits discovery or motivates a journey of thought toward further understanding and clarity.

I believe we can gain much wisdom by observing nature. Earth, as a university, remains forever open, extending its lessons to anyone who would attend. From the sermons of the sky to the lectures of the lands and beyond, I've been a student of nature over the decades, regarding Earth with curiosity, joy, and awe, all while being thoroughly humbled by nearly everything I see and try to comprehend.

This book is firmly rooted in those ongoing experiences and educations. My poems can be read in any order. Most of them can be called "nature poems" (poems about nature).

Other poems—those engaging environmental issues and topics more directly—approach what might be considered ecopoems or ecopoetry (ecologically-mindful poems).

After the poems, I've included a bonus "Reflections and Suggestions" section that explores Earth, ecopoetry, and related subjects. I also include a brief and friendly glossary of environmental terms I hope some readers find helpful.

I provide this entirely optional content for anyone who might like to travel further into these critical concepts and questions concerning our natural world.

If you're only here for the poems, that's perfectly fine, my friend. I'm just glad you're here. I welcome your company on this vital voyage from words toward truth, especially as we find ourselves amid one of Earth's most challenging times.

I hope you enjoy this book. Above all, I pray my words can do the Earth some justice and perhaps have the potential of inspiring someone to contemplate nature with a bit more consciousness, creativity, and compassion.

Wishing you, and our planet,
a lasting peace and wellness
and so much love,

Robert

Table of Contents

Part I: The Poems

Chapter 1: Return of an Earth Learner

To Earth, Old Friend

Earth of my youth, my long-lost friend,
whose meadows broke my reckless falls,
you brought me boulders, pine to climb,
smooth stones to skip across your ponds.

How much I miss those heedless years,
when we could play for days on end,
exploring fields with widened eyes,
inquisitively searching dirt
for earthworms, ants—such spiderwebs
and garden snakes and noontime quests
between the forest and the fence.
So few things seemed impossible.

I've not forgotten how it feels
to roll down hills or lunge from limbs,
plunge into puddles, mud, or snow,
or scan your nights for shooting stars

—bright memories as I reflect
on how you shaped my nature since.
It's been too long. I'm by your door
with many questions. Teach me more.

From Carefree to Caring

There was a time I didn't care.
For years I never sensed the dread
our planet might be ruined due
to human greed and negligence.

Then, Earth was backyard, playground, field,
a grassy hill to tumble down,
the space to frolic, trees to climb,
smooth stones to skip, a sky like clay
where I'd make shapes of every cloud
and watch them, dream, imagine, breathe
with all the freedom, peace, and ease
a child might enjoy, removed
from any fears this perfect world
was never indestructible
and could be broken easily.

But something changed:
I read. I wondered, heard the news.
Reluctantly, I understood
the world was not well everywhere.
In fact, it suffered silently
beneath a blitz of drills, machines,
the sawblades, waste, and wrecking balls.
Pollution. Logging. Creatures forced
to flee their lands and go extinct.
Then oil spills, the Ozone Hole,

entire lands erased to make
a way for "progress," "humankind."

As all this thundered through my mind,
I felt defeated, overrun
by every revelation met.
Who let this happen? Was it true?
How could it be? What should be done?

With knowledge comes the weight of worlds,
their gravity of questioning
and answers landing with a thud,
especially near one so young.

I had read some mythology,
of Atlas and the Titans who
rebelled against Olympians,
including Zeus, who punished him
to bear the heavens on his back.

I felt like Atlas since those days,
unable to shirk off the load
of everything I've seen and learned,
still shouldering the misery
of someone else's past misdeeds,
which keep me from relaxing much,
because it's now my burden, too

—and yours, because it's been bequeathed,
and no one throws this task away

as if it were a ball to catch
by yet another innocent
with little time to live carefree.

If Only

If only you would feel the wheat
  cascade around your sleeveless arms,
or find the river drowns out time
  with currents purged of memory,
or recognize the ants at work
  between the broken bits of earth,
or eavesdrop on a swamp at night.

If only you should ask the valley,
  "Swallow all my suffering,"
or have the mountains mentor you,
or learn the language of the woods
  and listen to their histories,
or watch the robin weave its nest.

If only you could let this wind
disperse concerns like seeds across
a field no one's paved or paced
  and then return with spring to see
  which ones burst into lavender.

If only you lived like the deer
that sleep beneath an evergreen
  and wake to graze the dewy grass
  that only knows to overgrow.

If only you became the rock

accepting every weathering
with stamina of centuries.

If only you flew like the eagle,
encircling the world with ease.

If only you lived naturally.

Earth Education

No school bells ring or busses run
to move us toward those institutes
of natural phenomena,
whose lessons might enlighten life

—if we'd be students just for once,
admit we're not quite teachers here,
between these heaps of plastic scraps
and deserts dead of negligence.

The lands forever lecture us.
This sediment's a syllabus,
as is the wind, the seismic waves
that shake us from indifference,

the beached whale and the arid hills,
attesting no one graduates
where errors never memorized
confer degrees of ignorance
whenever we have failed to learn.

Alumni of oblivion,
examine your calamities:

deforestation, toxic spills,
depleted sources, scarcity,
disrupted orders, species lost

with disappearing habitats
endangering the whole
unbalanced and unraveling.

Yet, education courses onward,
past our rampant truancy:

thick textbooks wait in riverbeds.
The ocean's deep with scholarship,
the coral calmly counseling.
The icebergs can instruct us, too.

Old impact craters still impart,
and fossil records will forewarn
of futures humans could avert.

See seasons as semesters now,
matriculation through the mountains,
forests of our furthering:

all earth's our university.

Among Wild Things

Within the woods, I'm lost and found,
a tamed heart among wild things
which thrive and drive where life compels.

My science—any structured thought—
seems stiff before organic branches
following no written path.

The urge of nature spurs the birth
of mushrooms, moss, the yawning fawn,
each rising vine and tuft of grass.

All boughs climb unrehearsed through air,
embracing sky, that vital light
without one lesson, map, or rule.

Yet order also flourishes:
there's balance, pattern, symmetry,
a course from seed toward canopy.

Past measurement and inquiry,
I sense collective, fine designs
of genius beyond intellect.

I'm of this rough earth, just as free
to study numbers, theories, schemes
—or let my teacher be this tree.

Birth of an Ecopoet

Among those heathered slopes that flow
down rounded hills toward grassy banks
along the river heaving leaves
around the crag and hazy bend,
much wonder starts when meadows end.

I'm blessed to meet this regal scene
of purple surges, speckled pebbles,
outcrops baring ancient stone,
whole mountainsides of evergreen
reminding me where I should stand

—not as a stranger who arrives
to claim and name some perfect earth,
commodify the natural,
then harvest sources harmfully:
I'm here to witness purity,

the untouched world so few have known,
this fertile floral realm of seeds
sown free by wind, unsullied, well.
If I just breathe, I start to see
the flawlessness: ecology.

Earth Learner

Earth, help me learn your world in me,
your courses of ecology:

why creatures need their rightful place
and vegetation seeks its space;

how habitats sustain our way
and devastation shapes the day;

where fossil fuels, born out of death,
imperil every precious breath;

when forests, mountains, meadows, seas
contribute to our histories.

Help us observe, respect, reflect,
conserve, correct, and to protect.

Please teach us to economize,
to balance, dance, and harmonize.

Chapter 2: Where Knowledge Buds

Sequoia Wisdom

Regard all roots. Guard knotted bark
grown bold and thick with history.

Lift up your limbs. Imagine them branching
a thousand times toward countless leaves.

Bring peace. Stand firm when lightning strikes.
Pray rain may always find the flames.

Lend ease and shelter readily.
Embrace your forest. Be the tree.

Flora, Restorative

Over rotted leaves and roots
and brittle branches cast aside
by forests dying for rebirth,
you spring ahead in sprightly dance
to reawaken slumbrous earth,

your liberated locks aswirl,
invigorating instant blooms,
while you may lean and leap to turn
through music none attend but you,
as grays grow rosy pink or blue,
and yellows, reds, and purples surge
in fields freed from winter's dirge:

so frozen waters flow from time,
birdsong quickens back to chime,
and foliage fills barren plains
where seedlings push past old remains
as death departs this vital rite
of evergreen and lavender,
when butterflies emerge to flight,
restoring beauty, hope, and light.

To the Susquehanna River

I've walked along your swerving shores
on mostly perfect weather days,
observing ripples cross the sky
you've mirrored in your muddy wash
while breezes calmly blur your tide.

I've seen you narrow, swell out wide,
caressing forests on your way,
tree roots wading in your shallows,
broken branches in the drift,
as leaves glide off like little boats.

You stream in peace, in slow retreat
from all the riot of the world,
although you've fumed with turbulence
and overflowed the bloated banks,
whole bridges, byways, placid berths.

You have your rapids, hoarded rocks
ensnared inside your endless ebbs.
You often wander like the sea,
as vast and nearly merciless,
unbridled at your very worst.

My photos never caught your core,
your dignity, vitality.
I've captured water, shimmering,

a trace of motion, scenery.
Your character escapes the lens.

To know you, if there's such a thing,
demands respect, pure vigilance,
that patience of eternity,
a selfless mind to swim your heart,
and only then we'd glimpse your art.

Symposium of Life

No branches groan.
The wind sits still.

The leaves lean poised
above the hush,

but don't read peace as silence here:

there's conversation everywhere.

These trees are speaking.
Plants confer.

Light chatter filters down through vines.

The dirt's alert with rich discourse,
while scented warnings tinge the air
informing neighbors of some loss,
disease or drought, intruders near.

All nature hums past human ears,
articulating messages
with chemistry,
pure energy,
electric networks,
stems and roots
exchanging news and nurturing

—life verbalized without one word.

Ecology 101

We're dozing off in class again
because we've heard it all before

—pollution, balance, habitats,
ice melting, carbon, rising seas,
endangered species, acid rain,
the overfishing, trees, degrees.

Perhaps it's mere redundancy,
sheer disbelief we'd wreck a thing
magnificent and vast as Earth
that leaves so many skeptical.

When lectures and semesters end,
we'll dream we learned or soon pretend
we're finished and the schooling's done,
forgetting every test to come.

Lavender Ambition

Wild lavender just lives,
just lives:

it neither seeks significance
nor needs to mean beyond one life.

Existing is enough,
enough:

not once it dreams to seize the field
or overtake the lake or hill;

there's much ambition in this living
purple surging spread by winds,
which sow its seeds by chance as far
as winds deliver seeds toward earth
permitting rootage,
flourishing

should rainfall follow warmth and light

and lavender return again

that butterflies sip nectar more
then hummingbirds come hovering
and raccoons consume all the rest
which gives to live and loves to live
—just live,
alive
enough for life.

Ecclesiastes of the Earth

The season of deep reckoning
approaches Earth with minutes left
to contemplate these cruelest truths
which jeopardize this fragile sphere
that bears the cracks of hammering
and all the dust of disregard.

We've time—no time—to undertake
the sum of what remains at stake.

Impossibly, we must address

the failures trailing our success:

the greenhouse gases trapping heat,

dissolving glaciers slowing seas,

gaunt polar bears on thinning ice,

the plastic islands, toxic waste,

more noxious smog and urban sprawl,

increasing needs for energy,

the oil spillage spreading death,

the fossil fuels and landfill rot,

environments consumed by greed,

ruined habitats, lost synergy,

resources nonrenewable,

the overfishing, whaling, hunts,

endangered species near extinct,

obliterated coral reef,

eroded soil, acid rain,

the pesticides and GMOs,

new deserts which were fertile grounds,

the drinking water going scarce,

particulates and nanotech,

deforestation, fractured shale,

diverted streams and mountains mined,

afflicted rivers, beaches closed,

the char and scarring of our wars,

protective measures overturned,

ecologies erased with ease,

few courses to conserve the rest,

denying science and the math,

the unlearned lessons of the past,

the tender balance tipped at last,

the second hand advancing fast.

Chapter 3: Reading Natural Histories

Millenary Evergreen

One thousand years—ten centuries!
What have you known, grand evergreen?

Your timeline frames a world of change:

the Inquisition, printing press,
Copernicus, all Shakespeare's verse,
the Renaissance, explorers, wars,
enslavement, every fight for rights,
Apollo missions to the moon,
the plundering of mother earth

—upheavals even while you climb,
lend shelter, lead these youthful woods
with patience, grace, and tolerance
for every weather: steadiness
attesting strength, resolve, and growth
can come of calm and constancy.

Attribution

A boulder nestled in the ground
sits underneath a precipice,
as if this rock fell down from there.

I'm tempted to project a myth:

the punishment of Sisyphus,
who rolled his stone forever up
for it to roll back down the hill
repeatedly. Repeatedly.

But here it seems he broke the curse
of infinite futility

—until I find the irony
of doing what was done before,
through centuries of poetry,

referring backward yet again
instead of simply standing still,
observing what's before me now

—the actual, no fantasy,
no allegory overblown:

Earth's narrative
and not my own.

Ascent

With stony faces,
furrowed brows,
the mountains seemed to scowl at me
when, once, I sought some magnitude.

But, after falling,
learning loss,
I understood them thoroughly
as ancient kindred, family:

we're sharing in
this climb of life,
from pressured earth and trampled lands,
to move above all worldly strife.

Efflorescence

Arise from mud
   with yawning
     arms.

Awaken, rise
   from seasons,
     dreams.

Relinquish instants,
   ages,
     space.

Become the lotus
   blooming:
     grace.

Mostly Water

The brook walks home with me again;
its gentle waters match my pace.

It eases me, my thoughtful friend,
who knows when I've much on my mind.

The brook sings soft but buoyant songs
and taps light rhythms onto rock.

Sometimes it brings me golden leaves,
reminds me of the perfect sky.

When rainfall comes, it loves to run
and skip and splash between the trees

then dares me to be young again,
to flow and go more naturally

—at least in mind, lest I forget
I drift like it through life and time

and stream beside it, toward the new;
for I am mostly water, too.

Breathing

A conversation shapes this wind,
quick whispering or questioning,
at times a crying no one hears
because we say these trees don't speak,
that rocks are heartless, voiceless, numb,
that water, cause for untold lives,
has nothing of a life or mind,
and then the rest is cold and dead,

the cloud's abstract vocabulary
dismissed as mist and meaningless
since we've not learned to speak in rain,
don't think how thunder punctuates
whatever lightning tried to write
so urgently throughout the night.
It's simply physics, we're convinced.
Suggesting more personifies,

as if the rivers had no wish
or oceans wrote no histories.
Those days I pass an evergreen,
the elder maple, oak, or ash,
I know their roots reach deep and grasp
this fertile earth more than I might.
Believe the breathing mountains thrive,
and all our cosmos comes alive.

At One's Disposal

Imagining: to be that tree,

    the one cut
    down,

    so young,
    undone.

How high
and wide it might have stood

    with leaves of gold,
    deep reaching roots,

    strong branches
    home to woven nests.

Instead, it's toppled, overgrown,
unfit for timber, firewood,
though home to mice who do not know
this forest will be cleared today
in preparation for more stores,
more fast food, gas pumps—many roads
of our making and unmaking.

Continuance

Some older petals ride the wind
then settle in the valley, gray,

but blossoms lend exuberance,
suggesting spring outlives its day,

although we'll know continuance:
new buds rush upward, through decay,

preceding season vanishing
when yet another heads our way.

Colorado River Wisdom

Five million years of sheer persistence
coursing through its arteries,
this river chisels,

skims and whisks
in millimeter increments

across the plateau,

ancient stones
eroded slow

while fissures vein,
cleave into grooves that form the gorge:

Grand Canyon's chasm widening.

From tributaries to the sea,
old wisdom's lodged deep in this rock,
aged sediments of ancient truths
deposited in caverns,
cracks,
abandoned hollows,
vacant days
where surges urge deliverance
past impasse toward complete release:

those wild flows just nature tames,
reshapes, retains,
lets swell beyond
our inclinations of control
and stagnant dams of human thought.

Come listen to the canyon now:

it gathers every echo, yes,

returning cries,
our causeless calls,

but have you heard its poetry,
its history, philosophy?

It vibrates with the river's voice,
which testifies to patience, grace,
devotion, motion, diligence

—that hardness shall be worn away,
ground down,
diminished
over time,

not with disorder,
forces,
war,

but subtle currents,
pressures welling

till they shake

and soon persuade
the rigid it may slacken,

lapse,

oust boundaries,

become the path
to send whatever means to stream
and liberate or saturate

through barren valleys,
fading lakes,
the splintered deserts of the earth,

or feed what heals,
must congeal,

immerse,
inter,

or resurrect
what's dying to be borne again.

Chlorophyll

This vital green tints everything:
the plants surround us, tether us,
enfold our world with foliage,

for nothing will outgrow the earth
or hold life never factors here,
behind these screens and sterile walls.

All's rooted in this grassy ground,
the breath of leaves, new oxygen
for arteries, inflating lungs

sustaining brains and framing birth,
from dawning thoughts for songs and words
toward bird flight, fire, snow and wind

returning waters through the skies
with rivers, oceans, rain and crops
resuscitating lives to rise

beyond the spectrum of our eyes.

Emerging World

Around a star beyond our own,
a planet blooms like early Earth
and stirs with signs of mild life
that's tenuous, microbial,
obscured within the murkiness
of land and magma taking shape.

The atmosphere there's nowhere near
the skies we fly: it's thicker, rich
with hydrogen, not oxygen.
No plants or trees arise and won't
for many million years ahead,
if they will even get to grow.

Development trends everywhere.
It's early. Dawn. And dangerous.
New planets may be forming, too.
At least a billion years can pass
before more life takes root and spreads.
Until then, hours brim with risk:

a comet could come crashing through
releasing seas of fatal change,
or asteroids reset the clock.
No galaxy gives guarantees:
a black hole or exploding star
can sabotage the sum of this.

Perhaps that planet lasts as ours,
eventually evolving beings
who'll question someday if they stand
alone among the stars, or if
more worlds like theirs exist in kind.
May Earth be something they might find.

Freeform

Yes, nature may arrange itself
in orders of geometry:

    organic shapes,
    the straightest lines,

    reiterations of designs,
    curvaceous turns of ratios,

    recursive forms we presuppose
    show structures, repetitious laws
    conforming to our formulas.

But nature's aims branch off from ours,
    diverge from urgent human hours,

    will fracture patterns we foresee
    with chaos, vague complexity

    escaping logic, calculus,
    all sciences and prophecy

because it lives
and must run free.

Grace

As I pause here, right at the edge
where land meets stream meets thriving life,
I'm tempted to make metaphors,
strike likenesses, and versify
the natural with mannered words.

These lenient waters, gleaming stones,
melodic birds, and vibrant woods
diffused in mirrored pastel skies
provoke me to suspend good sense
and scrawl more lines of poetry.

But I've not come here to transcribe
my fitful visions into verse.
Today, the trees and all appear
just as they must, within their place,
and I must learn from nature's grace.

Chapter 4: Animal Academies

Ornithology

Bright birds,
who raise me from my somber days
with vivid plumage, vibrant serenade:

how I regret
not studying your names
and never learning ornithology.

Each day
you teach us, "Witness. Savor. Hear."
We'll watch you, if we do, and maybe cheer

when you
give wings to beauty, music, grace,
then send your songs throughout our silent space,

inspiring,
if fleetingly, our minds
to fly beyond some pale and dying place.

At least
I prize your priceless company
and know extinction follows apathy.

Blue Warbler

Of course, you do not sing for me,
still I attend your soloing,
your conscientious serenade
originating past the pine
and echoing beyond my yard

—to whom or where, I do not know,
although your song—your aria—
flows fierce and fast upon this wind
with trills and crisp soprano notes.

I hope the one you sing to finds
this bright recital thrilled with life,
its undertones of solitude
—emphatic lyrics, subtle pleas
or promises, perhaps a love.

Whatever spurs these urgent bursts
of crucial music through the noon,
may all your calls and warbling
be heard, sweet songbird, clear and soon.

In Search of Animal Spirits

A dolphin swims my TV screen
and leaves an effervescent trail
before it leaps up from the sea.
I'm thinking, yes, that's much like me,
spinning, clicking with the pod,
but then I never learned to swim.

The show's host, off in China now,
presents a full-grown panda there:
the kindly titan chews bamboo,
seems quite content to pass the day
beneath the leaves in peaceful bliss.
I sense a wisp of him in me.

The program tours Galapagos:
a giant tortoise guards an age.
He scrutinizes steadily
then ambles past a mossy mound
with weathered armor, vigilance,
an admirable stamina.

Now mustangs charge the camera,
let nothing shake them from their chase
of freedom over open earth.
Yes, that's more like it: how they bolt,
unbridled, never broken in,
outrunning wind, nostalgia, time.

I binge-watch documentaries:
how speeding eagles seize a sky,
or elephants defend the herd,
the huddled penguins clutching eggs,
the hummingbird or bumble bee
encircling most perfect blooms.

I'm neither tiger, wolf, nor snake.
I'm tame, could never claim to take
my cues from owls, bears, or whales,
or anything of scales or tails.
I'm nature's student, taught to see
my spirit must be *modesty*.

Jurassic Tableau

Ferocious speed and thundering:
Tyrannosaurus rex breaks through
colossal brush which cannot hide
the crown of the Triceratops
now cornered between boulders, bones,
the scraps of the last savage feast.

Above, four Pterodactyls soar,
their leathery wings spread wide against
thick wind tinged with volcanic smoke
as glowing magma flows like streams
beyond the Stegosaurus herd
assembling at the river's edge.

A Brachiosaurus cranes its neck
to graze on leaves no others reach,
except the nearby Brontosaurus,
which lumbers in with booming steps
engraving craters in the mud
and crushing all inside its stride.

Velociraptors scatter fast:
an Ankylosaurus slams its tail
to ward off would-be challengers,
as if its armor's not enough
to disincline some hungry beast
from trying to bite through those spikes.

At night, the lands know little sleep
with roars and scores of gnashing teeth
preparing to defend or lunge
at anything that crawls too close.
The earth itself gapes wide to gorge
with oceans of devouring.

At the Bird Feeder

arrowing sparrows

   rattled grackles

  blue jay delayed

   onrushing thrushes

  pilfering goldfinch

the robin robbed

Bestiary

As you dispatch our habitat
to introduce new eateries,
oh, what a feast of ironies!

Consuming grounds to gratify?
Subtractions as you multiply?
Securing to endanger—why?

Polluting balance where you sweep,
you chase us, so we flee and leap!
But then, it's no man's land to keep.

Know, somewhere, in this upturned dirt
squirm unseen creatures, which, when hurt,
may, by their absence, soon subvert
whatever plans you might have drawn.

Perhaps another age may dawn
with wonder where your billboards yawn:
who were the humans? Are they gone?
Then Earth will answer, then move on.

To the Ants

I marvel at your diligence
your nests
and superhuman strength,

your unity, communities,
that you build bridges
with yourselves.

Yet some of you oppress, enslave,
wage wars,
and practice tyranny,

exterminating expectations
humans ought
to follow you.

Red-Tailed Hawk

Across the road from where I live,
perched firm atop a telephone pole,
a red-tailed hawk sits motionless,
determined in its patient wait
as it scans every inch around:

first earth, then trees, surrounding air
for twitching fur, a flick of wings,
a squirming tail behind the brush,
some unsuspecting squirrel, mouse
unfortunate to crawl in view.

Sometimes the hawk soars high above
in sluggish loops, friends with the wind,
though also there its watchful eyes
examine every trace of prey
that dashes, scrambles, darts, or stirs

—and then it happens straight away:
abandoned grace and coolness lost,
the red descent with talons outward,
swooping, scooping, quarry snared
—a mix of instincts, pulses, death

—all feral shocks of life unleashed,
reminding (after we've returned
to pillowed beds and quilted sheets)
that wild things are happening
just as we sleep and dream of peace.

Meerkats

Two upright sentries scan the sky
for raptors, anything with wings,

as three more cautious guards stand up
and sniff the air for jackal, fox,

potential threats while foragers
explore and claw through desert dirt

in search of spiders, scorpions,
the rare egg, lizard, root, or fruit,

whatever gains the gang a day,
preserves them from becoming prey

until they hear the warning sound
and run for refuge underground.

Flight School

The creatures teach us endlessly,
if only we'd attend their school.

The woodpecker would lecture strength,
persistence at the hardest task.

The owl counsels vigilance
through night, when sleep has blinded most.

The geese would plead, "Respect the seasons.
Welcome autumn. Wait for spring."

The bats encourage, "Use your voice
to find your way around the day."

The falcon's challenge: to excel,
to reach the speed no one can catch.

The peacock cheers, "Be radiant!
Show off your colors to the world!"

The ostrich heartens wingless souls
to find another way to fly.

The songbirds urge, "Be musical!
Bring melody into this life!"

The starlings impart unity,
the grace and greatness of a team.

The seagull shows us, "Ride the wind,
but seek your safety from a storm."

The robin, eagle, swan, and crow
would also tutor what they know

if we would learn before they go.

Caterpillar

Inaudibly
  you crawl about

eating

  slowing

seeking

  knowing

one day you shall climb on high

  transform

gain wings

  then shake the sky.

Butterfly Sight

Dim visions inched
among low stone

then crept upon
florescent trees

until each reached
its chrysalis,

transformed,
achieved lucidity,

emerged with wings
and soaring thoughts

transfiguring
the world to be.

Symbiosis in the Sea

A model creed of mutuality
reciprocates rewards beneath the sea:

remora join and clean the starving shark,
which leaves them food and speeds throughout the
dark.

The sea anemone protects and hides
the hermit crab for nourishment and rides.

The coral reef and algae also give
essential energies for each to live.

A pistol shrimp will shelter and befriend
the goby fish, who lingers to defend.

So naturally these creatures educate:
survival means we must *collaborate*.

Interdependent Independence

Bald eagles veer, ascend then glide
above the rapids, over clouds,
into the canyon, back again,
embodying pure liberty:

to soar and see, to breathe, become
without aversion, doubt, restraint,
while skies supply a boundless world
inviting wonder, wanderlust.

We see these wings but not the wind
the rising thermals, every force
delivering deliverance,
—the hidden prices physics pays.

So rivers reimburse the lands,
and oceans labor endlessly
that waves may break upon a beach
and whales can breach and hum their songs.

All freedom's deeds need energy,
the synergy of unseen things,
cooperation, harmony.
No independence comes for free.

Flightpaths

Two birds alike
in flight and height

crossed paths (one east,
one heading west;

the first with wind,
the next against)

—in destinations, most opposed—

but who could say
that would be it,

those counter courses
wove no more

or several times
surprisingly.

Do birds believe
in destiny?

Arias

I'm sure, someday, we'll say we know
the chirps and caws of every bird,
what they've been saying all these years.

Perhaps we'll find, they're much like us
gossips, critics, worriers,
full of news or table talk.

Perhaps we'll hear their shopping lists,
their pet peeves, or their evening prayers,
their favorite birdbaths, or their names,

or what they'll say about our house,
the neighbor's cat, the way I laugh,
the tree once home to many nests.

I'm sure that could be interesting,
possibly informative,
conceivably embarrassing.

I've wondered why my truck becomes
their favorite target when it's clean.
Although, I won't need to know.

Each morning I attend their songs,
their arias, whole operas.
I never understand a word,

and yet I sense those notes I heard
were beauty's music, peaceful, free,
and that's more than enough for me.

Hibernation

Entombed beneath the ashen snow,
the land looks perished, laid to rest,
but hearts beat on beyond this wake
of solemn hills and somber clouds.

Defying signs of dormancy,
a silent thriving spurs the dirt.
Stand still: the stillness disappears.
Expectant deer graze by the stream.

New cubs come stumbling from dark dens.
A white hare flees a famished wolf
distracted by the startled fox
that spots a leaping owl swoop.

In truth, few creatures savor sleep.
And nature cannot wait for spring
to ring in seasons of rebirth:
a restlessness enlivens earth.

The Hummingbird as Instructor

The hummingbird: it flits and sips
nectar from the blossoms' tips
and darts around before we blink,
anxious for another drink.

In feathered flurried blurs of light,
it navigates our garden: right,
then left, back up, then out,
precise, concise, without a doubt

a creature teaching us to make
the most of moments, what we take,
not to tarry, waste an hour,
to hasten yet attend each flower.

Milkweed to Monarchs

Just off the road, before the stores
can dream of cheapening this view
divinely ranged for royalty,
I wait for you, my rarest friends,
hoping wind will drift you here,
where I and all my kin remain
with welcome leaves and nectar rich.

With every day you don't arrive,
I wonder did you make it through
and blame myself for being off
the route you chose this spring around.
If I could free these roots of mine,
I'd take my chances on a gust,
if just to meet you in your quest.

Some think you frail. I know your strengths,
that grail you seek above that grace.
We bloom beyond all beauty's jewels.
With hardiness we both survive,
true partners proving they will strive
to rise where others stoop to dive:
alive so life renews to thrive.

Owl Optics

With vision piercing waking dreams,
the owl seems quite wise to us,
its pupils ever studying
beyond what shadows cannot teach

—although those eyes don't move as ours.
Instead, the owl spins its head,
resolves vague details through the dark:
extraordinary vigilance!

Some say the owl's color-blind,
observing mostly shades of gray.
We'd see essential lessons there,
outside old myths and metaphors.

How owls ground us in this light,
to question senses, what we'd find
past hindrances of human sight
—and what flies nightly through the mind!

Bear Bistro

Positioned, patient, plump, prepared,
the grizzly sits as if the stream's
become his table while he waits
for one more salmon to be served.

Now nature's like his waiter here,
where he's become a regular:
same seat reserved, no menu sent;
he always craves "the usual."

Fish fly into his jaws held wide.
He feeds until he's satisfied.

Accord

Birds keep treaties
with the trees,

or so it seems
with stones and streams,

the earthworms, dirt,
and everything.

But why?
What for?

They fighting war
with unity and synergy.

Whale Song

Blue whales, old Homers of the seas
with epics and mythologies,
ascend from depths and histories
to breach and breathe their ancient rhyme,
invoking muses lost to time
to narrate tales beneath the tide.

At moments, sorrows seem to rise
from the oceans of their eyes,
but then they soar up toward the skies
—what quests and ages they must know!
Their song continues long and slow,
the waves, their pages, where they flow.

Chapter 5: Natural Philosophies

Observing Orders of the World

Find wild lightning in the leaves,
diverging patterns leading light
throughout the stems and little veins
like tributaries branching off
like arteries like limbs of trees
like lines in palms like cracking eggs
like marble marks like fractured ice:
the smallest plans reflect the rest.

Survey the mountains in the clouds,
whole coastlines etched in jagged rocks,
the honeycomb in flakes of snow,
the nautilus in budding roses,
ocean waves of sound and wind,
whole hurricanes in galaxies,
recursive neural universe
reordering chaotic turns.

These features speak of vaster math
and chances set on reasoned paths
outside of accidental routes,
beyond all error, gamble, doubts:

the world abides by laws of cause.

Such symmetries should give us pause,
inspire wider wonder yet

of parallels we never met

in mirroring of scenes unseen,
to trace their natures,

what they mean.

Apologies

Forgive me, Earth—

    your hallowed lands

    your waters, fauna, flora, skies

—for every wretched verse I meant
to celebrate your stateliness:

    No roses blossomed beautifully.
    Colossal hardly honors mountains.
    Your oceans outreach fathomless.
    Horizons rival glorious.

Until deserving words arise,
I'll reassess my heedlessness
and praise you through
my speechlessness.

Evergreen Friend

I find a friend in all that grows,
especially the evergreen,
the one who will remain with me
once everything slumps underneath
the weighted blanket winter drags
across the land grown slumberous.

The evergreen's up late with me
when restlessness suspends all sleep
and I'm outside, beneath the stars,
to watch the dark absorb my breath,
the Great Bear yawning lazily,
reclining, soon to hibernate.

I cannot cool until spring comes.
I must keep moving, doing, dream,
remember, relish, not forget,
not yield to the stillness yet.
The evergreen emboldens me
to weather my mortality.

Mirror of Eternity

Sometimes, while staring at the stars,
I'll recall I'm a part of that,
the lavish cosmic tapestry
of galaxies and nebulas,
the black holes, all the gaping void,
the icy comets trailing dust,
each planet, moon, and asteroid,
our blazing sun, this very earth,
involved, atomic, just like you,
enfolded in the whirling whole
of what has passed and what will be,
though timeless, more than laws or mass,
significant, with consciousness
to comprehend the universe
is us, alive, quite self-aware,
inquisitive to know itself,
to search, discover, be explored,
with memories and revelations
if we can bring ourselves to see
its mirror of eternity.

Gaia's Alive

I press an ear against the earth
but hear no heartbeat, feel no pulse.
How could I, so far from the core?

I'm on the surface of the world.
At best, I scratch at fertile dirt
while I'm aware this planet lives:

it stirs, evolves, delivers, breathes,
speaks frequently if we would learn
its sermons, verses, ancient tongues,

the fractured grammar of the lands
and shifting syntax of the seas,
the winds inscribing histories.

Philosophy's within this rock.
These mountains teach. The rivers sing,
if only we were listening.

Earth Verses

Quick scripts of wind fill paper skies,

    long wispy phrases framing thoughts

   whose rhymes lie miles from my eyes,

  whole stanzas spanning continents,

   an epic flowing endlessly

    preceding any human word

     and of a tongue no one has heard:

  its eloquence illegible

until we learn to read Earth's verse.

The Earth Is Perfect...

...where *perfect* really means *complete*,
comprising every element
bequeathed by stars and cosmic laws
informing humble clumps of dirt,
which earthworms bore as ants collect
between the mossy bark and bogs
alive with frogs, bright dragonflies
that zigzag, vanish, hovering
by undergrowth now overgrown.

All's faultless and advanced out here
without so-called *developers*,
these realms removed from human trends
to level, asphalt everything,
betray the forests, then forget
this planet thrived for something near
four billion years before the saw,
the jackhammer and bulldozer,
our notion acres may be claimed.

No lotus knows the place or date,
and still it blossoms up from mud.
No mountain ever craved a name.
These creatures and the streams run free
past arbitrary boundaries.
No ocean sought authority.
How flawlessly the Earth revolves
without pretense, oppression, creed.
Such excellence stems from one seed.

Disembodied

More grudging ghost than mist, it seems:
the river's spirit quits its bed

yet wavers, stays reluctantly
before the haloed gates of dawn,

as if unready to retreat
before its lips kiss every sea,

though there is no denying death:
such exits merely mean return

through summer rain, chaste mountain snow,
cascades reviving vital streams,

baptismal waters purging hurt
or blessing once-divided souls

to seek peace in the healing whole,
absolved, evolved, resolved to be

embodying eternity.

Release

The last leaf
               breaks free
    from its tree

               then
          somersaults

     into
    warm wind,

          escapes the forest,

    fixity,

—a transitory liberty
until the tow of gravity,

where air gives way to weight and space:
no seasons left to face or chase

as settling turns toward, sleep, decay,
release from time and yesterday,
while leaving life for future, too,
so that the old promotes the new.

Sapling

Snowmelt and rainfall stream at me
with consciousness, cascading thoughts
beyond the stony precipice

toward rivers of insistent life
carved far across my canyon mind,

where cliffs exhibit sediment,
ancient beliefs, eroded knowns,
whole elemental histories

as rapids rage to reach the sea,
the oceanic mystery,

those islands I have never been,

new continents of flowering
alive with mountains, forests, seeds
sewn by the water, wind, and time

—then taking root to rupture dirt,

becoming saplings branching out
with limbs like mine embracing space,

the fullness and the vacancy,
tranquility yet jeopardy

when suddenly the dawning light
unshadows our earthly plight.

Fledgling

Embedded in this brittle nest
(which fittingly describes our world)
we take turns leaning near the edge
to glimpse or wonder what's outside
this crisp existence flecked with light.

With feathers incompletely formed,
we have it in our hearts to rise
beyond these woods, above the clouds,
then stretch these weak untested wings
between the valleys of the stars

—except we see no other perch.
It's early, though. There's much to know
about our lands, the seas, and sky.
Let's learn from earth, this tree, all life
before we try to leap and fly.

Natural Arts

I've tried to capture nature's likenesses
   on canvas, paper, sand, and blocks of wood,
   each portrait more a study of what falls
   outside the finer lines of mortal craft
   no matter how I might refine each draft.
We're painting canyons, prairies, creeks, the coast,
   volcanoes, glaciers, deserts, beaches, bays
   —thin surfaces, dead semblances at most,
   quick sketches, restless impressions that render all
   our illustrations entirely incomplete.
No paintbrush, ink, or pastels I'd apply
   can graze creation, spread the essence of earth,
   or blur the beauties lifetimes should express
   with deathless truths no artist could possess.

Genealogy of Breathing

Send forth your winds, forestal lungs!
Redeem our skies! Gift life again!

Come cleanse this smog,
these clouds of war.

Bring air for birdsong,
peaceful chants,

for protests,
cheering,
whispered prayers.

Repel the reek of industry,
these toxic gales,
volcanic dust,

what frenzied tempests we've compelled.

Raise murmured omens
undeterred
above the fog of apathy.

Disclose the scourges:
clear-cut woodlands,
timber blazing,

raving flaming avarice
endangering our family tree.

From roots to branches,
twigs to leaves,
lend us your limbs embracing all.

Please teach your genealogies,
the oxygen of histories

—how earth might thrive
when life may breathe.

Bracing Rays

With the plunging of this autumn sun,

    the season it delivers soon
    into the ocean's memories
    aflame with passion's dazzling hues,

let us remember summertime,

    those August loves, Julys of joy,
    audacious Junes, the Mays of haste,
    our Aprils of awakenings

    and Marches toward maturity,
    the Februarys of our fears
    and Januarys of all dawns,

when once again the sun may rise

    and thrill our eyes with bracing rays
    that chase old winters from our gaze.

Wisdom of the Mountains

The mountains brim with scholarship,
old wisdom shelved thick in the stone,
when we approach them modestly,
without presumptions of the world
to weigh us down before we start
our conscientious climbs to see
the blindness of supremacy.

Let pebbles boldly lecture us
in how the small gives rise to size.
Those slopes and boulders school us well
in inclinations and declines.
Respect the echoes, steps, and slips:
the sermon of the avalanche
is spoken once and suddenly.

Note fissures in the ragged range,
canyons, fault lines etched in earth,
yet oneness undeterred by cracks,
foundations that withstand an age
of weathering and gravity
as varied masses only add
significance to every inch.

May elevation leave us meek
so, when that panorama yawns,
humility resolves the view

and we'll not look down at the lands
but outwardly and overwhelmed
by every thing outside our reach:
the clearest lesson mountains teach.

Chapter 6: Through Roots of Truth

Forest of Momentary Gold

Ten magic minutes in the woods,
the sun struts through as if it's king,
one much like Midas, blessed or cursed
to touch and turn all things to gold.

Soon bark goes gnarled and dark again.
Bronze tones of earth and autumn leaves
return, enrich the brisk decay
with striking wisps of spectral life,

which dims once winter disenchants,
brings ordinary glory back:
the beauty of reality
devoid of momentary myths.

From Guesthouse to Greenhouse

At first our guest,
some warmth stops by,
stays for the day,
then needs to go,

only to find
blocked doors and hallways.
Trapped and tense,
it paces, phones

the front desk clerk,
and would return
its key and leave,
aware it's late,

unwelcome now,
too costly soon,
though no one seems
to take the call.

Fulcrum

High clouds like mountains call for awe

—but this branch broken over rocks
intrigues me more: how did it come?

Floodwater? Wind? A startled bear?

These sticks and bits have history,
significance and consequence.

No inch of this is trivial:

whole futures pivot on one stone.

Unrestrained

Expansive lands no hands have touched

—such overgrowth
and undergrowth,

waters bluest, deepest greens

all spreading without fences, bridges.

Hear breezes, songbirds absent machines,

no hints of roads or artifacts,

no powerlines or signs ordained,

just nature

plainly

unrestrained.

Maternal Earth

First mother of our fledgling world,
you nurture mountains, rivers, trees.

We coo and crash our plastic toys
and cast our bottles in the sea,

convinced we're better, all grown up,
and right to do as we would please.

Remind us to revere this life,
seek peace, and leave our gluttony.

Forgive us and admonish us.
We've barely learned our ABCs.

Come speak your earthly verse to us
so we may hear your poetry.

Teach us your ways. Sustain us yet.
Defend us from our vanities.

Course of Nature

Autumnal trees loom over me,
incapable of staying rain,
pernicious wind,
unsparing sun,
although
they
show
me:
breathe
and
strive.
Relinquish
losses.
Reach
out.
Revive.

Facing the Gorgon

Not one of us was Perseus,
not yet, when we were called to thwart
the demons surging from the depths
of negligence, pollution, waste
which threaten Earth (Andromeda
in this, the epic of our lives).

First, we, the heroes of this tale,
must brave the snakes Denial slings,
that Gorgon who could petrify
our spirits, hopes, then all of life
if we lose nerve, grow passive, go,
pretending perils don't exist.

Andromeda is on the rocks.
A great behemoth writhes and howls.
When generations yet unborn
look back upon our history,
what would they say? What will they see?
Our victory? Mythology?

Overcoming

The mountain knows of pressuring,

old welling stresses underneath
what once resembled peaceful fields,

which swelled and churned repeatedly
until those struggles ushered growth,

new heights above the ancient strain
to speak of toughness, tested strengths,
endurance over lesser things,

humility yet majesty
beyond all shards of fractured stone,
so mountain stands as more than rock,

much more than mass and aftermath
of unseen forces overcome:
it endures as our monument
of conflicts conquered and of time
defeated for a little while.

Bryce Canyon

No canyon:

amphitheater

geologic Colosseum

where gladiator elements
battle for millennia

their storied glories
etched in stone

epitomizing
blood and bone.

Ever So Briefly

New blossoms swell:

  their radiance

    erupts

      like supernova light

        through cosmic gardens
      dim with stars,

    where bright life

  briefly

wakes the night.

Mound

Nearby, all these little hills
seem every bit as tall and wide
as any mountain right behind them,

but one quick stroll, not halfway up,
helps me respect how distance sets
the record straight on what we see,

especially when arrogance
convinces me I've reached the peak
though I stand on a modest rise,

unlike these field ants I found,
who have no need for higher ground:
they humbly live from mound to mound.

Burgeon

The roses wait
for you to bloom,

to recognize
you, too, have thorns,

furled petals
over both your eyes,

which haven't grasped
all life's bouquets.

Arrayed

Outfitted in sleek worldliness,
we don our fashions cut from earth,
arrayed as one yet multitudes
unable to shake off the dust
from everything we're modeling.

With heavy elemental robes
we rove in vogue, snub nature's trends.
Our diamond eyes desire light,
the silken moon and velvet night,
some pearls of starry pondering.

Through gauzy veils of consciousness
we barely see the unity
adorning our humanity.
So few of us speak of design,
the patterned threads that bind us here.

We dwell on labels, tailoring,
though nature's fabric stretches past
materials, all time and space
—beyond the seams we tug and tear
when we outgrow the world we wear.

To Irises

Wide irises
(dilating eyes)

I read your fields,

realize

we're all like pupils

learning light

in college earth,
our school of plight.

Here, anything may graduate,

if by degrees, elucidate
the course of life

and future youths

toward wisdom through
organic truths.

Toward the Wisdom Tree

You're far beyond me, Wisdom Tree,
whose roots run deeper than all pain
and branches reach beyond my truths,
but I'll keep questing until death.

I thought I glimpsed you in the garden
just before I pulled the fruit
and took the first of many bites
of bitter pride, absurdity,

when Eden visions turned to soil,
deep furrows dug in earth, my brow,
where I'd sow trifling seeds of thought,
expecting harvests, sustenance,

not barren grounds of inquiries
besieged by droughts of intellect
or chalky storms of ignorance
to slow the growth of memory.

So easily you should be found
—your canopy climbs through the skies—
but I'm stumped here on lower ground.
So much escapes these foolish eyes.

Along the Shore of Surety

The ocean coached,

"Be like the beach!

Resist the tidal fears
which crash

like foaming breakers
on the shore:

those waves will scatter,
soon recede."

I'm now a student of the sea,
absorbing all it teaches me.

Cathedral Woods

Leaves, like stained glass windows, glow
as we step forth with reverence
into the forest of our prayers:

our place of truth, of comforting,
our exodus from worldly worlds,
revelatory sanctuary

where we give thanks for all that grows,
for what must die to fertilize
some future season to be sown
then harvested in autumn time.

A sermon spoken by the wind
advises we are meek but blessed,
mercified if merciful,
redeemed if we confess, commune,
receive this liturgy of light,
may consecrate and be at peace
with nature and ourselves at last,
long after fall and foliage
return us to our daily bread.

Chapter 7: Between the Teachings of the Trees

The Dawning

The ballad of the brook hums low
so nothing's rattled from this dream,
save early creatures weaving through
the undergrowth as waters gleam.

Strong sun slips in, dispels the mist,
revealing moss, weak doe, her fawn,
red squirrel chirping to her mate,
the fox about to stretch and yawn.

This forest dawns with synergy:
the zigzag paths of dragonflies,
mosquito fits, resourceful ants,
cicada code, young butterflies,

dead leaves, ripe seeds spread by the wind
—beyond the farce of "fight or flight"—
sustaining nature, seasons, Earth
while vital matters rise, unite

organic with inanimate:
essential soil, stone, and bone,
with bark and lark, the canyon, quark,
the mountain, pine cone, life yet unknown.

Reclaimed by Nature

Another gust kicks tiles loose:
they slide and drop toward shattered glass
of windows thrashed by last month's storm.

Green vines climb up corroded walls,
this shell of floors and offices
where birds and mice make homes today.

Cracked pavement and clogged drains confirm
old nature's on the move again,
reclaiming acres, inch by inch,

that land abandoned, razed of woods
to make way for new business firms
which since have moved and been renamed.

One sign, which once pronounced RESERVED,
clings to a rusting busted chain,
the lettered paint long weathered off.

The crows patrol the parking lots
as scrappy cats inspect the grounds
and seagulls watch from overhead

—the real landlords of this square.

Nature's Wordless Verses

Clouds as stanzas,

    rhythmic rainfall,

metaphoric flowering,

    rhyming waters,

haiku forests,

    lyrical moonlight,

sublime stars:

    nature's wordless verses rival
    our finest poetry.

Place

Slow ripples slip into the lake.
The clouds go almost motionless.

The stones contribute constancy,
and neither branches nor leaves sway.

From sodden edges, brush, to weeds,
it seems all things have found their place,

their corners of serenity
—except for me, the stranger here,

so wishing he could stay the day
but knows he should be on his way.

I linger for some minutes, though,
enough to settle, then to know

such peace receives me when I'll still
my vagrant thoughts and restless will.

Sapwood

I've moved so many times before
my early roots would learn the earth,
but here they're anchored deep and weave
round fossil stones and other trees
within this forest I call home.

Brisk winds could crack me years ago,
my narrow limbs left answerless
against the weather's questioning
—then fire, lightning, flooding, snow
entombing me before I'd grow.

Now toughened bark can stand the storm.
Concentric rings inside describe
my life of progress, year by year,
where hardy heartwood forms the core
and sapwood—fresh wood—adds more bands:

new layers of maturity,
of knowledge broadened, denser strength,
encounters, falls, and memories
which signify I'm still alive
to branch beyond myself and thrive.

The Last Tree Standing

The forest's one surviving tree.

Don't speak about resiliency,

development,

necessity.

Pronounce its name:

Catastrophe.

What the Tree Said

This sanctuary, it's my gift
to any creature reaching here:

    the owl, squirrel,
    robin, raven,
    bobcat, sparrow,
    hawk or cub,

    and any insect,
    wingless, winged.

I've welcomed every generation
with wide inclusive limbs

    encompassing
    from nest to death.

I've heard their prayers, their morning songs,
philosophies, mythologies
before they left.

So few return.

    So many autumns
    into springs.

Within this bark all claws or gnaws,

concentric rings (some thick, some thin,
some dark or light) have chronicled
each season suffered, overcome.

From foliage through obscure roots,
exhaling sky to fruitful earth,
I've witnessed - loved -
each breath
and birth.

Vital Deadwood

Another tree once towering tall
now falters, falls, creates new space,
may seem defeated where it rests,

but, in this forest most alive,
departure means arrival, too.

The bark corrodes, confers refuge
for possums, lichens, mice, and snakes.
Then shelter turns to sustenance:

old wood dissolves back into soil
for saplings, all emerging things

—succession, death as seasonal
between revivals and decline,
cold silence and warm songs of life.

Dewdrop

For all its smallness
(barely seen)
one drop of dew
can hold the world.

Sustenance

Consider pollen,
  tributaries,

pastures, cascades,
  breezes, breath:

how nature branches
  past all chance

to serve connections,
  nurture being,

togetherness,
  ecology,

feed neural circuits
  grasping earth,

the oneness sharing
  every birth.

Of Moss and Metaphor

Moss spreads, consumes another rock,
or draws its blankets over stone,
or clings upon solidity,
or animates the petrified.

I haven't quite decided yet:
devouring or covering,
some preference for permanence,
a resurrection of the dead.

Yet moss foregoes all metaphor
for shaded space, humidity
—conditions which will let it grow
beyond a moment's poetry

—like here, right now, across these thoughts:
that green bed lets my questions rest,
and, with no likeness left to wrest,
my mind can settle. Then I see.

Towards Tolerance

Their broadened branches intermeshed
  like silent couples holding hands,

these trees stand paired across our lands,
  some shorter, thicker, high, alike

or different, slim, yet similar
  how their embraces lift such love

above all human grasp or grudge.
  I feel no need to loathe or judge:

accepting life delivers me
  beyond dead fields of bigotry.

Yielding

The trampled path between these trees
erodes a little every week:
dead leaves and weeds, crushed grass and brush,
more crumbling limbs and saplings dashed,
remains and waste of wildlife,
cold stones cracked open by the ice.

Our scuffs gouge all that giving ground,
though earth reverses much in time
—not always toward what went before,
but instinct's there to heal, grow,
craft passages for things to come.
The journeys are not ours alone:

we share these courses with the world,
with intersections everywhere:
long corridors of water, wind,
gnawed bones, the thriving, thoughts unborn.
These yielding lands but guarantee
each footfall shapes this history.

Revolutionary Nature

It spins and twirls, returns or swerves,
   but "twisted" it shall never be,
this physics nature hinges on,
   from hurricanes or spiderwebs,
the whirlpool or the nautilus,
   the rattlesnake or artichoke,
to DNA, the narwhal tusk,
   the dust devils which pirouette,
the pine cones, roses, galaxies,
   whatever spirals into life.

No motives flow here, only cause,
   concentric ripples of effects,
as logged along the cosmic scrolls
   of orbits, loops, what veers toward earth,
how stars preside, where waves unfurl,
   which wings find flight or currents curl:
pure revolutions of no mind
   to free, create, destroy, or bind.

The Tiller's Tale

The ivy's on the climb again.
Another tree branch crashed my fence.
More weeds sneak back between these blooms.
My peaceful stream now overflows.
The dandelions thrive at will.
And then the cawing of the crows.

I'd wave white flags if this were war
because there's no way I could win,
but it's no contest, no debate.
I've mostly played the petty guest
domesticating bits of dirt
I'm said to hold but never own.

I've grown too old to plow the land,
too weak to dig a trench or well,
too smart to start another crop.
I'm ripe enough to know to stop
when nature claims the right of way.
I'll listen: earth has much to say.

The Improbable Rose

Consider every element
required to compose the rose:
that past, those many million years
of flourishing on early Earth,
uncultivated, lush, and free
to blossom far from human touch:

those gentle and defenseless roses,
meals for creatures who could feast
on open pastures unrestrained,
until the first of many thorns
would plunge in unsuspecting tongues
and send the feeders reeling.

Imagine what must come before
those foremost petals, stems, and seeds:
the atoms, light, and gravity
with physics of continuance,
improbable biology
perfecting beauty through the rose.

Chapter 8: Terrestrial Teachers and Sky Schools

American Falls

We've marveled at their ending acts:
the spectacles of waters lunging
headfirst from some precipice
toward gravity, the ceaseless crash,

this mist which blinds us while we stare
once more to gush about the rush,

now teeming streams storm lofty stone,
charge open air, take freedom's plunge
from stunning heights, then end the stunt
in moments grown perpetual:

upended eyes descend again
or downturned eyes ascending yet.

Who's curious what falls before?
Where tempered rivers give to rage?
How all this drama floods our stage
when metaphors pour off the page?

Faint rainbows grace the seething scene.
I pause to fathom what they mean.

Crash Course

The river schools
  the sharpest stones
through lessons on
a life refined,

 instructing from
  commotion's flow,

  a syllabus of friction,
    fish,

      erosion,
  rolling,

    drives aligned.

  The coarsest rock's well-rounded here,
becomes itself, gets grounded, bright
within the water's coursing light.

The Geode's Secret

Externally, an average stone,
abrasive, caked in dust and dirt,
so overlooked and left alone,
until what's masked becomes overt
when riven shell gives into light,
then pressure enters and reveals
what lies beneath this husk of blight:
exquisite crystals time conceals,
those treasures (never evident)
divulging deeper mysteries
no surfaces can represent.
These geodes shatter guarantees
that eyes alone should see or say
where beauty's truth goes on display.

Conceit

Clouds lose and gain familiar shapes.
I tease out similarities:
the swan or mouse, an elephant
whose coiled trunk becomes a snake.

It's entertainment, simple tricks
of finding patterns I impose,
innocuous imaginings
which dissipate in thinning wind

—unless I let myself digress,
presuming earth prefers designs,
wants definitions, nouns and names,
the unrest of our structuring.

One hidden danger here would be
ignoring pure reality,
neglecting nature's plainest states
as we invest more human traits:

our tendency toward vanity,
to paint our views on everything
instead of noting what's right there,
along the water, land, and air.

Dispatch

While winter strikes the woods again,
subduing trees and stone with snow,
the stream plows onward, through the frost,
determined like a courier
dispatched with certain urgency
to carry words—imperatives—
which must arrive, be heard in time,
as if our world depends on it.

Each letter here delivers life:
the need to feed and be a source
that serves the earth along its course
down mountains, mouths, through every gill
and thirsting roots that find their fill.

May every message make it through
and bear good tidings of the new.

Resemblance vs. Reality

It takes me days to draw one tree,
then more to make some mountains right.

The clouds and rivers drift and shift
before I might describe their light.

But nature paints with grace and ease,
leaves instant beauty everywhere

—no likenesses: reality
beyond aesthetics and compare.

Shells

Waves arch like pages flipped by winds,
which read the sea's anthology,

the verses turning in the tides
of undulating utterance

collecting moonlight, metaphors,
whole continents of imagery,

unnumbered volumes bound by time
unraveling when they may reach

the beach of meanings, where most words
leave lovely but such empty shells,

mementos, what we took for deep,
while poetries the oceans keep

flow fathomless, beyond the sand
of anything we understand.

Anonymous

While many think to christen it,
the mountain never craves a name.

All nature wakes anonymous,
escapes descriptions of the day,

and recognizes everything
shares in one true identity:

this universe our minds divide
in places, faces, claims to fame,

because we yearn to stand apart
and dare not sense we are the same.

Dramatic Irony

The clouds (like curtains) part as stars
appear before our lazy daze
as we respond with faint applause
and wait for someone entering.

But spotlight moon points down on us,
revealing us as characters.
We've never been the audience:
this drama is, in fact, our own.

For all our stages, scenes, and props,
what of our plots? Direction? Lines?
Where shall we enter, speak, or leave,
now earth attends our woeful show?

Rock Concert

Lightning strikes a power chord.

Thunder drummer.
Thrumming bass.

Ferocious notes storm everything.

Now raspy rain leans in to sing.

Frenetic night electrifies.

The concert rocks us,
shocks the skies.

To an Onion

Thank you for reminding us

all things have layers

(as does life)

—and,

(where we'll peel)

we may find

more tiers of truths

beneath each rind.

Corolla

Aesthetic,
also purposeful,

this petalled crown
the flower wears:

grand hues and scents
which fascinate

so monarchs gather,
pollinate,

perpetuating
majesty,

succession
in this dynasty.

Whole

Where sea meets land:
we call this "coast,"

the shores and borders, cliffs and sands
dividing countries—continents—

which oceans seem
to drive apart

—until you peer beneath these waves,
ignore the water, see this land

spreads on and on
around the globe,

revealing earth's continuous,
united, one, unbound by names,

where even islands
wed the whole

and any other line was drawn
by longing, war, or politics.

Scope

No matter how
I crane or strain,

my eyes cannot
contain the sky.

Things figure further
—scenes unseen,

undreamt of worlds
beyond my scope

—and though I'll only
reach a few,

their presence lends me
endless hope.

Walden's Nowhere

Sometimes, while driving,
I'll spot a modest little house
—a cabin situated near a forest,
a hilltop cottage by itself—
and I might recall Henry David Thoreau,
his experiments in detachment
from modern conveniences and materialism.

I'll try to imagine
someone like him in such a place today
living without television, Internet,
a radio or telephone,
no "hindrances to the elevation of mankind,"
as Thoreau put it.

Back on the freeway,
I'll hear news or songs mixed with static
(none of the celestial music Thoreau revered),
then find my exit,
eat, gas up, or shop some more,
as Walden's nowhere close to here.

Absorption

Between the stern dirt and the sea,
the shore seems lenient, yielding.

With incidental history,
our steps and leaps imprint the beach,

which bares the human weight of change,
how easily we impact things

without intention, much attempt,
just as we're shown the brevity

and irony in all we've done:
our consequential feats erased,

though unforeseen significance
in rearranging grains of sand.

The ocean goads us back toward land
to ground ourselves in firmer earth,

while waves persuade us to return
and learn what we've yet to absorb

from tolerance, life's influence,
recurrence, and impermanence.

Deliquesce

If rocks could speak,
some might admit
they've envied snow:

  those weightless flakes,

  the chance to vary,

   hover,

    grow,

     or simply melt
    away in time,

  back to
unassuming earth.

Resolve

These trees release their last few leaves,
   but do not grieve:

     this is not death.

No tree conceding coldness wins
   or forfeiting

     defining breath,

this is resolve, defiant life,
   tenacity

     to weather all,

the rest preceding wakefulness.
   Ascendancy.

     Don't call it Fall.

Cryogenian

No vehicles. No snowplows yet.
The roads have turned irrelevant.
The only sound comes from my breath
while I review the shrouded grounds,
the face of nature masked again.

The pine and spruce with elder elms
disrupt the wintry cover-up.
Already deer now reappear
to etch fresh lines across the field
with lanky legs and frolicking fawns.

There's silence yet, whole hours hushed,
as if the world was laid to rest.
Elsewhere, conflict slaughters days,
and chaos, flames, or tyranny
annihilate serenity.

I once read of our "Snowball Earth,"
some time of ice, the longest calm,
our frozen globe where life survived
—a blazing hope against the cold:
no winter has a lasting hold.

Mass of Life

The artificial trees are gone,
boxed with their tinsel, toppled balls,
entangled wires, figurines,
yet something has not wholly left.

Past crumpled gift wrap, bows undone,
drained plastic candle batteries,
tossed wreaths, discarded greeting cards,
know something faithful perseveres.

If only you would walk this hill
among the firs adorned with snow,
beneath these planets—real stars
which wink but never fail to light—

I think you'd find it there tonight
or sense it somewhere in the air
beyond the dark, the burning hearth:
this festive scent of evergreen,

nativity of squirrels, bears,
the holly, cardinals caroling,
the mass of life inside this wood
in close communion with the good.

Annals

Recorded for four billion years,
thick chapters of earth history
collect within this layered rock
anthologizing whatever was,

from fossils, fire, flooding, floes,
to weather, quakes, eruptions, mud
of generations, centuries
accumulating days of change
still chronicled throughout these hours
transcribing us, what we have done:

each step a stanza in this stone
of every action petrified,
preserved with annotations read
by anyone surviving us.

What will our volume say in time?

Shall others come to understand
our scrawls and scratches in this land?

Will we inspire or enrage
with what we write upon this page?

Unopposed

The trees are not my enemy.
No mountain stands to be your foe.

The desert's not our nemesis,
and no vindictive winds will blow.

Yes, nature wages storm or drought,
an earthquake, plague, eruption, flood,

but none of that is personal,
political, a war for blood,

just physical phenomena,
unbiased forces start to end.

The oceans never fight the sky.
I see the river as my friend.

Salvage

Down overgrown, forgotten roads,
deserted dwellings tombed in grass
(with doorways repossessed by vines)
have hallways cobwebbed, rain-soaked stairs,
infested spaces, molding rooms,
warped floors turned into termite food,
and shattered windows framing ruins
which time and nature may reclaim
if possible and purge that dirt
of negligence, poor tenancy,
extravagance, and toxic plots.

Now bats and birds repurpose roofs.
What thumps one hears come from the hooves
of deer and creatures home again
to nose through ash and scattered trash.
New rust and dust appear with weeds
inheriting abandoned lots
while signposts slump and saplings stand
where mechanisms once bled ground
and wildflowers might abound
should life return to injured earth
with hope of healing and rebirth.

Chapter 9: Land Lectures and Water Courses

To Be More Like the Waterfall

To flow with nature,
glow, and know
the way of life so openly
with urgent purpose
surging free
beyond all rocks, into the wind,
reviving,
mighty to compel,
or smooth, or soothe, or move, sustain
what must lunge past
the edge to plunge
without delay or doubtfulness,
or retrospect,
remorse, or fears,
just coursing forth, alive, decisive,
progress towards
futurity,
more buoyant, deep to lift and drift
if grace,
embracing gravity,
may blend, descend, transcend, or mend
with lucid
continuity.

Drowning or Diving

I can either

    enter an ocean
    feeling insignificant,
    overwhelmed by its enormity,

or

    realize,
    when I dive into the sea,
    I'm part of something greater yet.

Reach

The ocean loves me once again,
sends gentle kisses on soft waves
which seem to grovel at my feet,
as if to ask me to forgive
the waters for the other day
when they rushed at me all at once
then tipped my easel in the flow.

I know the ocean's not at fault;
it breathes in peace, but then the moon
provokes its tides from high above.
The sea and moon portray a love
I've painted: pressure, gravity,
two yearning worlds kept far apart,
what lone desire won't possess

—a question rolling through my art:
how do you reach and keep a heart?

Currently

High tides
        rise inward,
                waver, wane

  in cycles
        time has
               lost track of:

  life's ocean
        flows
             unknown
             to known,

  before the beach of what will be,

  beyond the reach
of what we've seen.

Endurance

The woods are full of broken limbs,
small branches twisted off by wind,
the ruptured trunks of lightning strikes.

I've see trees fallen, caught, and braced
by other trees with hardy arms
embracing them for years to come.

The canopy conceals ruin,
and foliage disguises loss.
Yet there's revival, healing, hope

in pine cones, acorns, walnuts, chestnuts
germinating as we speak,
new sprouts between decaying leaves,

more saplings nourished, flourishing
as they gain footholds, strive toward light,
root further into sturdy earth.

Each moment's death here marks the birth
of something, beyond wound and strife,
that dares to last and sustain life.

Painting Earth

Astonishing, these sweeping scenes
one landscape painter can portray
with details down to blades of grass,
rose petals, leaves, a textured stone,
or sometimes vines, a distant deer,
red berries, pine cones, drops of dew

—particulars escaping eyes
of someone like me somewhere there,
high up a hilltop, humbled, gripped
by everything I cannot touch,
geography unreachable,
whole mountains framing Painting Earth

—that fine art nature shapes with ease,
without a draft or final stroke
because this picture never ends.
Each step reveals even more.
I shift but inches, then I see
the meadows of eternity.

Bankrupt

Another wave deposits trash
in vaults of sand once lined with gold.

These banks of our impoverishment
keep ledgers of expenditures,

those resources we've overdrawn,
bad trades with nature, debts unpaid

for bottles, mangled plastic, glass,
long statements rating deficits,

miscalculations, liquidations,
profits risking bankruptcy

of earth, existence, sky, and sea.
Who will admit insolvency?

Green Space

It's heartbreak watching two deer graze
along this swarming city street,
so far from their true habitat,
which all this was not long ago
before plans to "revitalize"
turned woods into an urban park,
a "green space" tamed and orderly
with benches, tables, walkways, pools
installed for human recreation.

A squirrel hurtles past trash bins
as pigeons rove and poke about
while joggers take another lap
around a sitter with three pugs
distracted by an apple left
beneath the swings where children leap
into the grass cut every week.
It's well-kept, yes, this paradise,
this Eden of our sacrifice.

Oceanography

Reversing currents scurry, blur
as breakers race,
dissolve again

across the shore
where we were dense
so many waves from yesterday,

when you first taught me how to drown
my ignorance
within this sea,

assuring me
reality
survives those momentary ebbs and flows.

Though I've come back to roam our coast
with little wisdom,
this I find:

the ocean holds
cold obscure truths
which scarcely reach our warmer beach,

so now I'll go and dive below,
risk sharks and all
to seek and know.

Family Circle

I see much kinship with these trees.
When young, I'd leap inside their leaves,

imagining how it might be
to stand on roots instead of legs,

embracing earth and rising high
with steadiness, a certain strength,

this skin as rough and tough as bark
and limbs of wood, no longer flesh,

held wide, collecting golden light
while perching birds rehearse their songs

or fly, return, to weave new nests
since I've become a sound abode,

a formal member of the forests,
accepted for accepting them,

remembering I'm part of this,
the lineage of plants and beings.

Now older, I can say I know
all life entwines, and we must grow

together, nearer, clasping hands
as family across these lands.

Lake Meditations

I. The Lake as Painter

Imagine lakes paint what they see
—the flowers, clouds, the hills, each tree—
in concrete forms, when calm, or more
surreal or abstract when moved:

then mountains soften, marbleize,
while forests smear green leaves through skies
and boulders wither blissfully
as all the earth blurs beautifully

—until some stillness quells this art,
and anything that's flowed apart
regains composure, wholeness, light
within the water's steady sight.

II. Like Lake Placid

When tempests rest, dense clouds depart
with all their thunderous stunning fear,

and once again this weathered heart
begins to ease, my mind flows clear.

Then, like the calm lake, I reflect

more placidly upon our world

its tranquil beauties to respect
and meditate where madness swirled:

why lightning strikes at things unseen
as muddy gusts besmirch and scream

where seething rain did flood the land
that trees collapsed where they stood grand

and how mist hides the mountaintops
or frost destroys the last good crops.

To breathe, at peace with life and light,
embracing change with steady sight,

composes me so those who'd peer
across these waters see the deer

the geese and wheat, the peaks and plains,
the hint of fish and distant trains

each mirrored nearly perfectly
within this newfound clarity.

Picturesque

Perhaps you've found a *perfect place*
in your excursions—pleasant grounds,
some sanctuary nature framed
as what one might label *picturesque*.

In all my walks and drives I've seen
so many scenes inviting me:
a stream that weaves the woods with life,
or ponds like mirrors to the stars,

old mountains that have outstared time,
expanses grand, vast majesty,
beguiling blooms spread hill to hill,
long grass like hair combed by the wind.

It's tempting to veer off the path,
encounter splendor nearer, but
there are such fine lines drawn between
the outing and incursion, yes:

one step too far, and then I raid
that flawless painting of the earth.
I've learned to pause, take photographs,
zoom in without disturbing things

—just simply witness, not disrupt
birdsong recitals, drowsy deer,
the milkweed's drunken butterflies.
I leave in peace so peace abides.

Hydrologic

The waters never hesitate,
express no questions on their way:

they know to flow, to speed or slow,
around, below or over, through,

instinctively from high to low
toward gravity, until detained

—and even then they'll spill at will,
persist, infuse or inundate,

eventually evaporate,
ascend, commence to circulate

as rain sustaining life and all.
Lives rise because these waters fall.

Above

Like arrows launched from autumn's bow,
ten thousand geese arc over clouds,
descending slowly, south of us.

Then spring returns a smart barrage.

Slow motion war? No. Nature's rites.
Survival. Life. No mindless fights.

The Steady Flowing

The water knows where it must go
around, between, and over stones
preserving streams for centuries
with rigid purpose, weight, resolve
directing flows through
firmer earth,

unmoving so the rest may move,
as motions crave a stable base,
resilience rocks avow at once,
affirming certain stamina
against all weather,
pressure, time

—that covenant of constancy
between the change and changelessness
which balance turnings of the world
with permanence compelling life's
essential progress
over death.

One

No grain of sand or blade of grass
exists within a solitude.

Just ask the ocean's water drops,
the waterfalls or morning mists.

Approach the mountains of the rocks,
these teeming ants and swarming bees,

the seasons, fruit, the seeds of seeds,
the wildflowers and the weeds,

the woods of roots and boundless leaves
—they shall affirm this plainest truth:

not one thing stands detached, alone.
Know everything, from thought to bone,

runs unified from earth to sun
toward stars and cosmos. All is one.

Chapter 10: The Perennial Education

Inception

An orphaned fawn pads warily
between the hazy lake and woods.

It's dawn, though dark and desolate,
these grounds once safe a day ago,

until some hunter aimed and claimed,
beyond a doe, this innocence.

The young deer steps toward morning sun,
begins to brave what has begun.

What's Not Here

It's what's not here that strikes me most
as I hike past the highest pine
then turn to face the yawning vale
framed by old firs on either side
and mountains bathing in the sun:
the earth allowed to be itself.

I've never seen so many deer.
Perhaps the sparrows sense it, too,
that absence of what contradicts
this lush and untouched countryside.
I hear just wind, and what a thrill
to witness nature live at will.

Ode to the Ordinary

Let's celebrate the routine things,
the growing grass, some bird that sings,

how clouds shall pass as squirrels fret,
those mundane matters we forget

when wind drifts through the leaves or chimes
or raindrops rush a million times,

the ocean's motions, seagulls, beach,
warm sand, a hand, a seat, a peach.

Revel in sunrise, starlight, moon,
the everyday gone far too soon.

Winter Solstice

On this, the longest night of nights,
the cosmic clock ticks silently
between the pine and Perseus,
the sycamore and Sirius:

all constellations stay their course
as heavens wheel leisurely
and Jupiter descends again
behind the hilltops hushed with snow.

We have good cause to celebrate,
us lovers of the summerly:
each hour heralds spring's return,
anticipates great radiance,

until June brings the briefest night
and autumn leaves us lesser light
—revolving seasons, sun and earth,
from utter stillness toward rebirth.

Naturally

The waterfalls
   autumnal leaves

   descending sunlight
shadowing:

how every thing
   obeys its pace

   and right on time
falls into place

without me doing
   anything.

   How easily
the skylarks sing!

Garden Promise

The promise of a garden? Growth,

though nothing swears the budding runs
proportionate to sweat and tears.

Our efforts and those blooms diverge

much as branches of these trees
will follow no specific paths

from toiled soil toward the sky.

Now time reminds us nothing may
coax golden roses from these thorns.

So glories in their mornings rise
according more to June's caprice
than perfect weather, states, or hopes,

confirming us, our humble part,
and nature's ever-changing art.

Reclamation

These properties
we briefly lease

across the acres nature lent

eventually
get repossessed

by earthquakes, floods,
a system stressed,

eruptions, weather, drought, decay:

the terms of earth
that bind our day.

Renewal

The deer, who never fully leave,
now roam free where the snowbanks thawed,
deliberate, with softer fur,
gently stepping through the field.
Some fold their legs, lay down to rest,
exemplify serenity,
while others gnash fresh tufts of grass
along the corners of the creek.

The squirrels swerving through the elms
may never live contented lives,
suggesting that no season's safe
and we must ever be prepared,
as foragers, uncovering,
recalling what we've come to hoard,
and that there's little time for sleep
if one intends to see more springs.

Plump robins bob on branches, dart,
sweet harbingers of earth's rebirth,
hopping, singing, searching, perching,
flapping, landing, seizing worms.
The muddy ones expecting eggs
will nurture nests in just some days,
weaving, leaving, circling back,
devising for the births to be.

For all these creatures, this is life,
though they can be our teachers, too,
instructing us in modest ways
to set aside our nonchalance
then never waste a summer day,
but cherish every renaissance,
greet blessings with more gratitude,
and, from the struggles, be renewed.

Nature Study

We often think of nature as another entity
and talk of coral, clams, and whales
as separate from land and sea,
apart from dolphins, waves, and skies,
the deserts, canyons, waterfalls,
then every thing our eyes comprise.

And yet, we're nature—us—as well,
and share in life, this world, the stars
that turn within the carousel
we've come to call the Milky Way,
which spins with other galaxies
inside this cosmic interplay.

The universe that binds us all,
it lives, is conscious, full of sight,
from quarks to any leaves that fall
across the rivers, though the light:
creation flows in you and me,
unites us now, eternally.

War on Nature

Green fields seem like battlegrounds
as mechanized divisions mass:

first excavators, dozers, cranes,
with loaders, rollers, lifters, mixers,
harvesters, and tractors, plows,
then dump trucks, graders, pavers, rigs.

No boulders will oppose for long.
The trees resist most peacefully,
their silent might soon overcome
with nothing one could call a fight.

The planners term this victory
—impediments erased with ease,
objectives met, resources seized,
the wild tamed, a land renamed—

but, under tar and wet concrete,
prevails good proof of self-defeat.

Agreement

No ocean hopes
to slow the moon.

No mountains think
to stay the sky.

No star defies
the rest of space.

So I must flow
and know my place.

Growth Rings

Inscribed inside these ancient stumps
long-rolling tales of centuries

reciting climates
deluge
droughts

infestations

vicious bouts
of windy shifts

infirmities

corrosion
coldness

injuries

conditions whispered
every band

historians of limbs and land
their chronicles our own concern

how chainsaws razed
or forests burned.

Epiphanies—how nature sings
and centers us within its rings!

Garden of Early Delights

Not quite the garden labyrinth
(few hedgerows, roaming hyacinth),

yet here I wander, far from squares
of concrete routines, flights of stairs,

and straggle loosely through this green
where lavender and lilac lean

as tendrils bend toward coiling vines,
near blazing blooms, the scent of pines

past branching paths inviting rounds
by running fountains, flowered grounds,

the birdbaths plashed and songful calls
of wind chimes, distant waterfalls,

rejuvenations, turn by fern,
reminding me how much I yearn

to pull back from that brute array
of urban furies, where I may,

so nature soothes my rattled heart
and I might learn more from earth's art

much like Thoreau did years before.
We all need Waldens to restore

that younger wonder, precious zest
we forfeit once we're repossessed

by duties and delays each day,
until those moments we can stay,

attend those lessons ever there
within the roses, waters, air,

behind that shrub, beneath these leaves,
the rising lotus, while light weaves

more luminous beauty with dim eyes
so they may waken, recognize

these gardens will be grayer soon.
When autumn comes, love life like June!

Spiraling

In
seashells,
pinecones, galaxies

the
spiral
gyrates endlessly,

from
Jupiter
to ammonites

by
tempests,
Fibonacci sums,

in
whirlpools,
golden ratio,

to
tendril, tail,
staircases, snail.

Branches of Knowledge

The forests know of
letting

go

releasing
leaves

so to survive

resisting winters
to revive

what winds and freezing
cannot seize.

Let us be students
of the trees.

Thank You Note

My gratitude's inadequate.
I should salute parades of rain,

the spiders, flies, each blade of grass,
the leaves and weeds now everywhere,

the raucous crows, when roses sting
or snowfall closes everything.

Yes, let me thank ambitious squirrels,
pregnant deer behind the elms,

the raccoon searching through the shed,
the songful crickets, cardinals,

the heedful hawk and wary hare,
the barking dog three houses down,

the stubborn stones that stand their ground,
the furtive fox, where vines surround:

all plays its part on life's grand stage
in ways we've yet to grasp or gauge.

To Future Students of the Earth

To learn what wisdom nature holds,
mute all internal dialogue.

Look past old notes then listen close
to lectures spoken by the stone.

Read textbooks authored by the sky,
thick dictionaries in the dust.

Become a student of the earth.
Mull over boulders, floes and flames.

Reflect on water, falls and streams,
the ocean's cyclopedia.

Seek teachings in the coral reef,
volcanoes, icebergs, canyons, rain.

There's institutes of insect life
and animal academies.

Watch wildflowers cultivate,
the mud and mountains mentor you.

These forests are philosophers,
the roots of truth and scrutiny.

Part II: Reflections and Suggestions

This *entirely optional content* is intended primarily for readers, nature lovers, aspiring environmental champions, and anyone else who welcome some more thoughts about Earth, ecology, and ecopoetry.

Just as with my poems, these entries can be enjoyed in any order.

Part II: Table of Contents

Reflections

Suggestions

1. Some Earth Words Worth Knowing
2. Some Poets of Nature to Explore
3. Nine Notable Names
4. Fifty Earth Books to Consider
5. Websites for Further Exploration
6. Crafting a Creed for Earth
7. Earth Empathy

A Relatively Brief Observation Several Billion Years in the Making

In a universe measured in *billions* of years—around 13.8 according to NASA's *Universe Exploration* (universe.nasa.gov)—and on a planet estimated at 4.5 billion years old, modern humans (*Homo sapiens*) have inhabited Earth for a tiny fraction of that time: 300,000 years, according to Smithsonian Institution's *Human Origins Program* (humanorigins.si.edu).

In that time, humans racked up quite the record, inventing many impressive things: agriculture, communication, music, art, mathematics, architecture, transportation, television, computers, rocketry, and robotics, just to name a few. Those achievements attest to the vast potential of human imagination and ingenuity, but they only tell half our tale.

Regrettably, humanity's history includes many sinister chapters: war, slavery, inequality, colonization, tyranny, genocide, environmental disasters, and more. Desolation cannot be humanity's legacy. Suffering cannot be our purpose. Coexisting peacefully with Earth, its resources, and all forms of life must become our topmost priorities—and soon—if we are to prove humans *deserve* to survive.

As of 2023, it's *not* too late, but we *are* cutting it close. We still have a chance to slow and reverse humanity's environmental injustice. To start, we need to be honest with ourselves and acknowledge the very basic math behind concerns of temperature changes and declining natural resources. With common sense and critical thinking, we could ask questions, learn about nature as individuals, accept verified truths, and advance ourselves beyond old debates. We have no time to waste.

If, somehow, we decide to stay with our current course and rate, doing little to moderate environmental impacts while we accelerate our resource consumption, this brutal truth should humble us: Earth *has* done without us, and it *can* do without us. Even an unwell, post-human Earth would continue to orbit the sun indefinitely, and the cosmos would *not* grind to a halt in our absence. If we're going to be small-minded, we'll forfeit longevity.

On the cosmic scale, 300,000 years is rather *momentary*. It's a number that *seems* impressive when compared with human life expectancy, which, as of 2023, is nowhere near 100 years, according to the National Center for Health Statistics' *FastStats* (www.cdc.gov/nchs/fastats). That brevity partly explains why so many people approach life, and Earth, without a long-term vision. Life *is* short, and so *we live*, with few hours and little mind for the roads ahead or left behind. We often live *for the moments*—our minutes, our trivia, our fleeting dreams.

And yet, that very kind of short-term and self-centered thinking only allows long-term ecological issues to escalate worldwide. "So what? It's not *my* problem," someone might declare. Well, only so many people can say that until it *is* their problem, a worsening one inherited from earlier generations. Eventually, something like pollution can become *everyone's problem*. Once it does get to be too late for humans to mend their ways, Earth's situation *will* naturally, automatically, and tragically, become *nobody's problem*—until, perhaps, another sentient species succeeds us some day and evolves sufficiently to make its own case for continuance.

Befriending Earth

Earth is not our enemy. When storms surge, volcanoes erupt, floodwaters rise, and earthquakes shake up everything, it's nothing personal, certainly nothing motivated by malevolent motives. Very early on in its development, in a solar system wracked with collisions, Earth was a precarious and perilous place, completely inhospitable to life as we recognize it today. Earth was not yet a friend to life. That would change, but not before a long forbidding history of natural cataclysms, ice ages, and mass extinctions of prehistoric organisms. Still, none of that remotely qualifies Earth as an adversary to humans.

Nature—or, perhaps more appropriately, the *natural order of things*—involves a continuous series of physical events—*natural phenomena*—and the consequences of those results produce *more* events and effects. The outcomes can be devastating, of course, but that is simply nature doing what it does. From the summit of Mount Everest—Earth's tallest mountain—to the Mariana Trench—the deepest oceanic depression—our world involves a perpetually evolving system of interdependent causes and effects. Over billions of years, such global events eventually enabled early humans to thrive in a far more stable world no longer dominated by dinosaurs.

Today, certain habitats have seen disturbances or destabilization due to human activity. Some weather patterns are less predictable and may veer between extremes of cold and warmer temperatures, droughts and downpours, stagnation and hurricanes. Earthquakes and other natural disasters also gain our attention and remind us we live in a world where nothing is certain or to be taken for granted.

As we witness the damage caused by storms, it can be difficult for us to perceive Earth as a friend. Thankfully, we needn't look any further than Earth's uniquely qualified ability to host life for us to see it *is*, in fact, our existential ally—unlike unwelcoming worlds like Venus and Mercury, whose atmospheric and surface conditions leave them barren, desolate, incapable of nurturing life. Humanity exists, along with all the plants and animals, thanks to Earth's resilience and reliability.

Humans sometimes seem to lose sight of that simple yet vital fact, especially when their actions or inaction can endanger the environment repeatedly, or alter ecosystems in lasting and unprecedented ways, disrupting or destroying communities of organisms or entire species. Whenever human decisions impact nature negatively, nature's balance can be tipped irrevocably, endangering Earth's long-term ability to sustain life. This, in turn, imperils us.

Although we often regard that natural order from a distance—as if it were apart from us—it can be helpful, if not restorative, to recall *we are also part of that natural order*. We're inextricably involved with our world: when it excels, we do well.

Nature often reciprocates: if we become problematic toward the environment, it can trouble us in kind. Air and water pollution present powerful examples of that: air or water tainted by human activities can corrupt a habitat and surrounding areas, potentially contaminating other living things, including us, as we breathe that noxious air and ingest that same fouled water, indirectly or directly.

These consequences come full circle rapidly, revealing how humans can endanger themselves, even when that was not their intent. We sometimes forget *it's all connected*. All of it. Everything—down to atoms and subatomic particles—exists in a perpetual state of interdependence. Ecology, the study of life and its environmental relationships, helps us learn more about the connections and dependencies shared between organic and inorganic things.

A little familiarity with ecology prepares us to appreciate how organisms coexist, collaborate, and rely on things—and each other—to such extents that the disturbance or eradication of one organism or species can lead to detrimental or deadly circumstances for other organisms and their habitats.

As we continue to study Earth, we can learn more about these essential relationships and how they bind humans to this extended family of living things, this global community of communities. As we become more conscientious members of this planetary fellowship of life, we may become more encouraged—even out of purely selfish inclinations toward self-preservation—to see our planet remain wholesome and welcoming toward life.

If we approach ideas such as conservation, protection, and sustainability from that practical and universal perspective of self-preservation, we can see it's *not at all* a political position to wish our planet remains habitable, healthy, and continuously available for the benefit of *everyone*. Nor then could it be a partisan act to advocate for such things as Earth's wellness, or for the defense of endangered species, or for reduced pollution and better sustainability. When all else fails, we can recall this simple, objective, and indisputable fact: the Earth, on its own, is *apolitical*.

Earth has no nefarious agendas. Earth simply *is*. Every day, natural forces and living things shape Earth's reality and ability to sustain life. Earth has evolved and continues to evolve. We owe our very presence to that incessant planetary evolution. Collectively, though, we have not demonstrated great gratitude to Earth. For centuries, we have exerted our influence over the natural order, to such a vast and lasting extent that a growing number of scientists say we live in an era called the Anthropocene, the first geological era defined by human activity.

Humans have levelled lands, rerouted waterways, brought about large-scale deforestation, eradicated species, introduced unprecedented pollution that's left regions of the Earth in toxic states, impacted the atmosphere, and more. We've even managed to pollute the space around Earth, and that "space junk" can present problems to current and future space missions. Historically, humankind has not been the best of friends with the earth.

Meanwhile, Earth has tolerated shocking amounts of environmental transgressions, but there *are* tipping points and points of no return. Earth is neither immune nor inexhaustible. Its resources are not infinite. Mathematically, our consumption rates do not appear to be sustainable. Conservation is still popularly regarded as a movement instead of mandatory or mutually beneficial. From that alone, it would appear humans have somehow chosen to be more antagonistic than friendly towards the Earth, and the results of that ridiculous hostility can only lead to self-destruction when extrapolated over decades and centuries to come.

Sure, we can fantasize about finding or creating other habitable worlds, but even the latest exoplanetary surveys (e.g. The Planetary Society's planetary.org/worlds/exoplanets and NASA's exoplanets.nasa.gov) confirm remotely Earth-like worlds are very few and extremely far away. Earth is and will be, for *many* generations to come, all that humanity has. If we do expect to survive indefinitely, we must discover new and improved ways to coexist with ourselves and our world, especially as we all have a vested interest in mutual wellbeing.

Recognizing Earth as an ally, a friend, a colleague in the business of life, and as part of our family, could position us to think in more collaborative, sympathetic, and harmonious ways with the planet, its environment, and ourselves. To begin, we can start to step outside more, experience nature more consciously, breathing in fresh air, and taking a few moments to appreciate some area or aspect of Earth.

It should move us *to be alive*, to participate in this universe, this scientifically miraculous and improbable existence. What a welcoming world it would be if we'd recognize and then agree we were never born to suffer or to destroy, to subjugate or be subjugated, but rather to live, to coexist and collaborate with each other and with Earth. This peace begins to be attainable as we seed hope in many more minds, nurture awareness of nature, and learn to live more mindfully and responsibly with Earth.

With mindfulness, mercy, and humility, we could be better than friends with Earth. We could act like what we really are: a family. Imagine what would come of that.   Extending such careful consideration, such kindness, such empathy, and such love toward the Earth is altogether logical, perfectly practical, wholly humane, and entirely *natural*.

All our family trees, back to the beginning of life, have grown their roots in this good earth. Let us honor that organic truth that lives on through us. Let us befriend the earth again, as individuals, as communities, societies, countries, as friends, and as families prizing togetherness above division, life above death, and love above all.

Foundational

The Great Pyramids of Egypt, with their breathtaking bases and steady ascent toward the stars, demonstrate the importance of sound foundations. Many other ancient architectural sites, beneath the weathered rubble of their figures and fallen walls still have bases mostly intact. From our most basic architectural practices and principles—all tested over centuries—we know the durability of human constructions depends upon the materials employed as well as the methods and stability.

Whenever we look at Earth, do we observe its sturdiness? Do we perceive its trees as columns propping up the very sky? Do we regard the colossal groundwork bracing any mountain range? Do we discern the indispensable underpinnings of life—each rock, each root, each clump of dirt? Perhaps not as often as we should, because Earth's there, is always there, our backdrop and the ground itself, what keeps beneath our concrete, roads, our homes and playgrounds, walkways and parking lots—that elementary surface mostly overlooked, until an earthquake, sinkhole, flood, or other natural calamity forces us to face the very bedrock of existence.

Foundational to all of life is not just Earth, the world alone. What nurtures nature and supports it emerges from much smaller things: grains of soil, sand, fibers of wood, decaying matter, pebbles, leaves, what wind and rivers bring or leave, insects, microbes, seasons and their weathering, fine particles of everything, cohesion yielding constancy, solidity of unity. The mountains gain their grandeur from these finer bits, these elements that constitute the seen, unseen, and every last thing in-between us and the sky and Earth: the dirt, the mantle, crust, and core.

We want our dwellings to endure, our homes to cope with weather, time, the whipping winds, and not collapse easily or at all. These sanctuaries of our lives and storehouses of valuables were fashioned with materials of stamina, capacities to bear the weight of stories, walls, entire rooms of stuff, and rooves defending families, possessions, and our most precious things. We'd never want to compromise those structures that surround our lives and businesses. We cannot have fragility or threats of instability. We count on bricks, load-bearing walls, whole infrastructures holding firm.

We understand these basic things, these residential requirements, and yet with Earth—our one true home— we witness different attitudes, much willingness to rattle and raze, along with inclinations to make way for projects, lodgings, industries, more fast-food spots, another mall. Machinery of every kind is used to transform land each day and banish plants and wildlife from habitats where they once thrived.

Each ecosystem that's weakened or eradicated subverts Earth's constitution: what once existed and then vanishes cannot disappear without repercussions. Each absence triggers consequences we have yet to experience, comprehend, or regret. Instability can lead to many unprecedented and unknown dangers: unpredictable environments, unexpected climate conditions, and potentially more intense weather events that can threaten human infrastructure.

Earth's integrity and resilience emerged naturally over billions of years of steady challenges and changes. In our relatively brief tenancy, we've somehow found ways to fortify our lifestyles and entertainment options while weakening our planet to unforeseen extents. Now we observe, with some surprise, the chips and fissures in foundations bolstering the living world:

The Cracking from Our Pressuring

It's shocking Earth should be impaired
by something small as human hands.

How we were pounding all those years.
What were we thinking at the time?

Perhaps we figured Earth's so vast,
so strong, above all faltering,
or maybe we presumed our acts

of "renovations" through Earth's house
would only bring amenities,
increased convenience,
comfort, space, at least for us

—as if we could forget the rest,
the other tenants living here,

and all the things that count upon
so many other things unseen,
and all those things we overlook,
forget to shelter, lose for good,
when we get home then close the door
to recline in our living rooms
and settle in a mindless light.

Environmental Care = Love

I see caring about the environment as something that transcends social movements and political inclinations: it begins and ends as a form of love. This is not to be confused with *a love of worldly things*—the pursuit of purely material possessions and fleeting luxuries. Rather, I mean a *familial* kind of love.

From parental perspectives, caring for the environment coincides with the love of family: they recognize the wellness of the world is foundational to the happiness and health for their loved ones. To look at this from another angle: most of us could not conceive of any parent or guardian who would prefer a *more* polluted, unstable, and unhealthy planet for their children.

And yet, contrary to reasonable expectations of wanting to see one's family safe and sound, there are more than a few persons out there who vehemently disagree with any talk of environmental protections or any proposals to limit or eliminate negative human impacts on Earth. One can only hope they'd consider their children—or someone else's children—and ultimately prefer a pollution-free and stable planet.

Those environmentally adverse perspectives, and the decisions they tend to engender, exceed personal, familial, or political domains and bring real consequences to the rest of the world, even if that's not the original intention. This is how we all get to participate in our society's collective decision as to what kind of Earth we will leave behind for others to inherit.

For many of us, these choices are clear and easy: we would choose life over death, compassion over indifference, flourishing over destruction, wholesomeness over toxicity, togetherness over division, and peace over conflict. These *should* be simple conclusions reached without delay or extensive deliberations, but, as always, it comes down to what each of us stands for or against.

Of course, it's not always a choice between *A* or *B*. Life is nuanced with many gray shades between opposing views. Realistically, though, there are no halfway choices between a healthy or unhealthy Earth. We either conserve and protect, or we choose to endanger nature. We cannot be mindful to only some areas of the world while choosing to exploit, deplete, or possibly destroy the rest.

We either want all our children to inherit a habitable and healthy world, or we do not: environmental justice must pertain to everyone, not just to a favored and affluent few. We either pollute or choose not to pollute, wherever we could and should prevent it. We cannot occasionally condone the contamination of nature or ignore a problem when it's not in our back yard.

We either care or do not care: we cannot half-care, shrug one shoulder, or be concerned periodically, on certain days of the year, such as Earth Day. We either defend the environment, or we leave ourselves vulnerable. We either embrace sustainability or choose to consume natural resources and non-renewable energies at unsustainable rates. We either love or forsake Mother Earth.

On Ecopoetry + Nature Poems

Sunrises, trees, birds, flowers, oddly shaped clouds, and countless other things in nature can inspire poets to write "nature poems," which I would define simply as *poems mainly about natural phenomena. Ecopoems*, on the other hand, go further than contemplating nature: they maintain a consciousness of Earth while engaging environmental considerations more directly.

The *eco-* in *ecopoetry* has to do with *ecology*, as in *ecological poetry*. To appreciate what that means, we need to understand *ecology*: it's a science of how living things relate, from microscopic life to larger organic communities and habitats. Ecology helps us to learn about nature as we explore those connections.

More than that, *ecological poetry* openly examines the impacts and implications of humanity's dysfunctional or destructive relationships with Earth. In its most outspoken mode, *ecopoetry* champions environmental mindfulness and confronts the effects of human negligence and ignorance.

So many of our environmental issues stem from unawareness and our emotional and physical detachments from nature. Not everyone has a chance to experience nature's beauty or to develop a profound sense of connection with Earth. Here's where ecopoetry can help us reapproach nature, relate with it, and deepen our appreciation of all things natural.

Until people know about something and understand it intimately, they are not likely to care. While ecopoetry cannot, on its own, make people care, it *can* educate as well as provoke further inquiry and genuine interest. Education can reveal paths toward empathy. Ecopoets can encourage readers along those paths toward enlightenment.

Encouragement can take on many forms, many directions. There are traps and challenges along the way, such as politics, exaggeration, emotion, alarmism, and technical jargon. Nature is altogether apolitical, and any attempt to politicize it misses the point that Earth should be valued and preserved *by all the people, for all the people.*

Writers can sound legitimate environmental alarms without resorting to exaggeration or intimidation. However warranted, emotions can distract or overwhelm readers. Relying more on facts and less on feelings is to let objective truths speak for themselves. Ecological issues, once understood, should leave most readers concerned and urgent for others to know about these things—and to act soon.

Scientific terminology can cause difficulties for readers who are unfamiliar with certain concepts. Readers enter our works with a diversity of knowledge, vocabulary, experiences, expectations, as well as varying levels of interest, caring, and skepticism. All of these things factor into a reader's ability to comprehend and interpret information.

I believe it helps our cause as writers to make important points accessible to readers. With poetry, something too buried in abstract imagery, poetic language, or metaphor runs the risk of being overlooked or misunderstood by readers. Wherever readers have a chance to learn, they may be more prepared to participate in related discussions, debates, and decisions, and they can even help other people understand the environment better.

Ecopoetry can do all this and more, revealing humanity's ecological flaws while encouraging everyone to strengthen personal and community bonds with nature. If, at the very least, an ecopoem helps someone regard nature with a little more reverence, I believe it has succeeded. If an ecopoem can compel us to rethink our relationships and practices with nature, it has fulfilled its primary purpose.

Aligned with the natural order of things, the ecopoet has a selfless yet heroic role to fulfill: to speak, on behalf of Earth, using the right words at the right time to the right readers, whose awareness and caring could eventually grow to help "save the world" in some small or substantial way. To be an ecopoet is to love and defend nature *and* humanity so all life may continue to flourish freely, fearlessly, and far into the future.

Earth and the Universe

After looking well outside our solar system, throughout our galaxy, and even other nearby galaxies, scientists have found there is, so far, one and *only* one completely Earthlike planet they know of: our Earth.

Yes, thousands of *exoplanets*—planets beyond our solar system, around *other* stars—have been detected. There are *vaguely* Earthlike "terrestrial" planets, various worlds with land and roughly comparable physical compositions, unlike "gas giant" worlds like Jupiter or Saturn or an "ice giant" world like Neptune.

Some exoplanets orbit their stars in what's considered the "habitable zone," a distance that's neither too far nor too close to a star, so that water—an essential ingredient of life as we recognize it on Earth—could exist as a liquid, providing potential environments, substances, and sustenance for organisms that might exist there.

Planets need more than water to host and nurture life. An atmosphere is important, as it provides air and warmth and protects against harmful radiation from the sun. A stable solar system also helps, so that comets, asteroids, and planetary collisions are not constant threats. Planets with life also need to be located far from cosmic destructive activities like gamma ray energy bursts, exploding stars (supernovas), or black holes, which can swallow anything nearby.

Our moon has proved itself essential over billions of years: it is believed to have regulated and slowed Earth's rotations while influencing Earth's oceans (with some help from the Sun) through its nearness and motion, giving rise to tides, which make the oceans perpetually energetic and dynamic. Our moon also goes through predictable phases of illumination, lending periodic light to Earth at night, while moving in dependable cycles that helped humans to gauge time, seasons, and when to plant and harvest crops.

For another world to have exactly *all the things Earth has* would require far more than time or fortune. Earth's history, like the history of every person and living and inorganic thing on our planet, is unique, the result of pivotal instants and epochal events. No other planet, near or far, will have precisely experienced what Earth did during its formative years and eventful existence.

Long ago, during the "heavy bombardment" phase of our solar system, Earth and other planets are believed to have experienced countless collisions with comets, asteroids, and fragments jettisoned from other impacts for many millions of years. Our cratered moon openly wears its battle scars, the largest of which we can see on clear nights, when our lunar satellite mostly reflects the light of the sun.

The varied terrains, unique compositions, along with the singular natures of planets orbiting in our solar system—and any other solar system beyond ours—all affirm Earth is a cosmic rarity for light years in any direction. Now, having confirmed our planet *is* so uncommon, *so* extraordinarily hospitable when compared against other worlds, shouldn't we be moved to respect it? Shouldn't we marvel at it constantly and affectionately? Wouldn't we want to guard it with the greatest gratefulness?

I hope such knowledge of Earth and the universe would only inspire us to preserve Earth, its precious resources and ecosystems, and all its varied organisms, which developed and adapted for millions of years under conditions wholly unique to Earth, ensuring such life is to be found nowhere else. With some understanding of what it takes to establish a world such as ours—and knowing that *this is the one true Earth we will ever have*— we should all feel blessed to be here and alive, if not obligated to advocate on behalf of nature's wellbeing.

Long before we had rockets to travel into space, humans dreamt of reaching other worlds. Movies, novels, comics, and astronomy all fed the desire to see humans embark from Earth and sail the seas of stars. We may see someone standing on Mars in the years to come, and we will celebrate that grand achievement. We might also establish an outpost on the moon. Humans will eventually build larger space stations. These will be amazing things, but even the best of those efforts will not provide substitutes for Earth.

The reality of the universe interrupts us from our science fiction reveries of living on the moon, or "terraforming" Mars to make it more Earthlike, or floating freely in pressurized chambers as we gaze into space. Earth life really has nowhere else to go and thrive. Virtual reality and haptic (touch) feedback technology enables us to simulate and interact with Earthlike environments anywhere, but those are pixels, artificial light, pale and soulless imitations of the real thing. Why would we entertain settling for *that* when we already have Earth?

We should remind ourselves daily *there is nowhere else for Earth life to go but Earth*. We should remember forever that, in a universe rather *inhospitable* to life, Earth *is* an existential miracle, something never to be devalued, defaced, or treated as disposable. May that simple information live in us, thrive in us, center us in our efforts, make us meek, inspire us, shake us from our stupor soon.

Memento Vivere

May we remember how we live,
what we can't claim eternally,
and what we've lost or long misplaced,
and everything we would forsake
should nature bend to negligence,
the scourge of greed, our apathy.

Let us affirm the earth's our home,
our universal sanctuary,
abode of all inviolable life,
which vanity must not defeat.

And may we serve this sanctity
with mercy, steady reverence,
a humbled love, much gratitude,
as Earthlings, and as cosmic kin.

On Alarmism and the Environment

Once you learn of the full extent of environmental issues our world faces, you might be tempted to turn into a full-blown alarmist, but that won't help the environment much. In fact, it could make matters *worse*. Emotions often obscure facts and attract far more attention than the information you'd like to communicate.

Composure and logic don't always prevail, though. Sometimes we're so astounded by some inconceivable ecological disaster, such as an oil spill, that more abrasive words leap to mind. We might believe louder and more visible protests are necessary to gain attention. Sometimes we *do* need to use literal and figurative megaphones when our concerns get drowned out by disinformation and the voices of denial.

Shouting isn't always likely to win over the ears and minds of people we need to understand and to agree on the need for progress. It is imperative people hear us, though, and listen with a view to learn. We cannot run the risk of our concerns being ignored or misunderstood by those who may not share in our awareness or distress. Our concerns *are* their concerns, too, but they might not even know that yet.

As advocates of factuality and awareness, we need to remain focused, humble, collaborative, and compassionate—even among those individuals who do not yet comprehend the severity of environmental issues we face today. We can try various ways to reach them, but there are things we cannot entertain.

We cannot overstate problems or the implications of certain environmental indicators. Though humans *should* be concerned, we cannot employ fear as a tactic or make outrageous claims. Unadorned truths about habitat and biodiversity loss, emissions, etc., are usually unnerving enough when people learn about those things.

We must be truthful, matter-of-factly, civil, direct, inclusive, and community-minded. Then people can have a better chance of learning how something halfway across the world is relevant to them and influential elsewhere. As more people feel welcomed into this discussion, more of them may willingly participate in vital debates or decisions. And, later, they may even contribute to potential future conservation and protection efforts.

Some people *will* be difficult or seemingly impossible to reach. Many people already decided—or have been persuaded to believe—that the planet is fine, climate change isn't real, and environmental warnings come from agendas beyond science. Climate alarmism rarely helps these matters, and divisive partisan rhetoric has not advanced the cause of Earth. More than ever, we need objectivity, awareness, calmness, self-discipline, inclusion, and unity.

We need to move forward together. We need to think globally, to speak *beyond* borders, beyond personal persuasions and party lines. Ecological issues affect everyone, everywhere. We must acknowledge Earth was never naturally partitioned in "red" or "blue" regions, nor does nature exist in anything but a perpetual state of ongoing causes and effects: physics, chemistry, weather—natural phenomena scientists can objectively image, measure, and study.

Without scientific methods, we'd be stuck with opinions, emotions, and speculations no one could substantiate or try to falsify through precise empirical analysis and experiments. Science, with all its accuracy and objectivity, must be at the center of our ecological discussions and any proposed solutions. Making that science accessible is of utmost importance, too, I believe.

In addition to technical terminology and complex concepts, people also have to wade through an online world full of deceptions, outdated data, and other informational difficulties when it comes to learning more about the environment. We need to help people navigate these topics with greater ease so they can reach their own conclusions naturally. Without understanding, individuals and communities may be at risk of environmental mishaps. Public education is for everyone's wellness.

Many people might feel desensitized or averse to discuss things like pollution or endangered species. Certain phrases and warnings have sounded so often that such words may be disregarded. Still, we should try to educate as many people as possible. We need to nurture a basic but lasting consensus, a global majority of individuals who favor nature's preservation and humanity's sustainability over lesser options.

I'm optimistic that objective information presented in calm and clear ways will inspire more persons to develop environmental awareness willfully. Through provable truths, logic, basic math, common sense, and compassion, what we say about Earth should resonate far, with much magnitude, and be received with all due attention. I believe this will encourage many more individuals to embrace conservation and environmental protection as natural extensions of their newfound knowledge.

On Indifference and Inaction

Sometimes we settle for things as they are and don't want to get overly distressed about a situation if it requires exertion or dealing with something disagreeable. We might look away, procrastinate, hope things get better. This personal policy of avoiding conflicts can spare us from a few anxious experiences, but it does nothing to resolve troublesome circumstances. In fact, it can often make matters worse, leading to more tension and suffering.

There are things we might delay for a while, such as cleaning a room, fixing something mechanical, or paying a bill, but some things cannot be postponed indefinitely. And, while we might be unconcerned by certain conditions, especially if they're some distance from us or not seen as directly affecting us, it doesn't mean we're wholly removed from the predicament. In fact, we might even involve ourselves *more* and bear some responsibility for its continuance simply by feeling, saying, or doing nothing.

In a world where everything connects with—or depends on—everything and everyone else in some major or imperceptible manner, to say "who cares" or "it doesn't matter" may be relatively unwise and less than truthful. Everything we do or don't do affects our world in some way. We might not perceive it immediately or at all, but, since birth, we're active participants in this world, contributing energies and changes to it in ways we might not fully comprehend. Our actions and inactivity matter.

We might consider our feelings, speech, and silence even less impactful than our deeds or stillness, but they *are* relevant, significant even, at certain points in life. Our emotions or insensitivity can make a huge difference for us and for others. We may believe we are detached, that we are impartial, independent, and our emotions and thoughts are of no importance to others, but that is rarely the case. What we believe can factor strongly in any given situation, and our devotion to those thoughts guide or divert our deeds.

Human actions have roots in thought. Thoughts and feelings can matter more than we anticipate. We are part of something larger, something so interconnected, so inseparable that we cannot pretend to be unrelated, disconnected, alone, or insignificant. Each presence in this world is momentous. Physically, we have mass, weight, force, energy. We move and consume. We dream and do. We, and all living things, form a grand family with the earth.

Distant issues can affect us locally. Air moves. Water circulates. Animals and insects are ever on the move. Fumes and microscopic particles ("particulate matter") from factories can travel, as can smoke from forest fires and volcanoes. Environmental factors and mishaps can eventually impact our comfortable corners of the world, however remotely our dwellings might be situated.

Forget any talk of climate change for a moment. There are many other kinds of environmental issues that deserve our attention:

- Industrial pollution and accidents afflict the world (as reported by many, including the European Environment Agency: www.eea.europa.eu/publications/counting-the-costs-of-industrial-pollution).
- Long-standing forests are falling at alarming rates (as reported by many, including NASA: earthobservatory.nasa.gov/world-of-change/Deforestation).
- Food and natural resources are being depleted at escalating rates (as reported by the United Nation's International Resource Panel: www.resourcepanel.org/reports/food-systems-and-natural-resources)
- Air quality is a serious concern (as reported by the American Lung Association's 2022 "State of the Air" report, "Most Polluted Cities": www.lung.org/research/sota/city-rankings/most-polluted-cities).
- Natural habitats dwindle and disappear around the clock (as reported by many, including The National Wildlife Federation www.nwf.org/Educational-Resources/Wildlife-Guide/Threats-to-Wildlife/Habitat-Loss, as well

as Einhorn and Leatherby's article in *The New York Times*: "Animals Are Running Out of Places to Live," Dec. 9, 2022).

- Clean drinkable water is becoming scarce in parts of the world (as reported by UN-Water, www.unwater.org/water-facts/water-scarcity).
- Particles of microscopic plastic are infiltrating human bloodstreams (as reported by Vrije Universiteit Amsterdam in *Environment International*, May 2022) as well as oceans, waterways, animals, and food sources.
- More endangered species near permanent disappearance (as reported by many, including Elizabeth Kolbert in her book *The Sixth Extinction*).

That is quite a list, and it's just a sampling of the many issues currently afflicting Earth.

It's astounding to think Earth's wellness—and humanity's future—come down to someone caring or not caring, doing or not doing something necessary, speaking out or remaining silent on the environment. But it's true: collective human indifference and inaction imperil our planet and all its life.

When we *do* care about a crisis and at least *begin to wish* we could do *something* about it, we create hope and increase (ever so slightly) humanity's potential for betterment. Caring matters. It means we're no longer indifferent, perhaps even no longer content to be silent bystanders when some area or aspect of nature suffers from human negligence or destruction.

Why do so many people choose to ignore the topic? Why do some people seem so ready to dismiss science? There are many reasons. For example, some persons may have become desensitized from having heard dire climate warnings for years, so much they might automatically dismiss such talk as paranoia or a hoax. It helps to consider their perspective: when something doesn't happen as promised or prophesized, a certain degree of doubt is to be expected.

Accuracy is essential. Some warnings or predictions from previous decades may have been, in retrospect, premature, perhaps a bit overstated, or inaccurate. Technologies and sciences behind our most current environmental knowledge mature steadily and meet with international scrutiny, testing, and reassessments. A higher quality of information makes greater public awareness possible.

Other forces, such as defeatism, cynicism, and pessimism hinder some members of our global society from being more interested and involved. Often due to circumstances beyond their control, some people feel powerless, insignificant, convinced, unable to make a difference in the future of Earth. Some persons might be overwhelmed or just might not have time to study the environment due to health, economic, political, or other living conditions.

Someone might invoke the defense mechanism of denial to keep upsetting information at a distance. Some people may not have had a chance to develop critical thinking skills or to achieve open-mindedness to the point they can comfortably and objectively examine facts that may challenge their current understanding. Economies, social conditions, media, and other influences, along with personal experiences, all shape minds in ways we'll never completely fathom.

Since the state of the environment affects everyone, we do need more people to learn about Earth and care. How do we do that? We don't. We simply cannot *make* people care. Caring is a personal phenomenon, something that develops and deepens between individuals and the things or people they cherish. Genuine connections, interests, needs, appreciation, respect, and love heighten such values and cause something or someone to be regarded with reverence and seen as essential, priceless, beautiful, and irreplaceable.

Experiences can move us toward caring. Each individual walks a unique path. Not everyone gets to experience the exquisiteness of Earth. Some people were born into harsh social and/or environmental conditions. Anyone who has not had the chance to nurture friendly and loving relationships with the natural world may value other things entirely, or simply have little or no mind for planetary perils.

I'm grateful to have been able to encounter and enjoy nature since I was a child, having a sizeable backyard full of trees and plants. I got to learn a little about flowers from my mother. Rocks mesmerized me. Discovering caterpillars become butterflies or moths was astounding. Spending those hours outside helped me develop a lifelong love of nature and a profound sense of connection with it that is, all at once, physical, spiritual, philosophical, poetic, musical, artistic, and as dynamic and organic as Earth itself.

As I reflect on those green and joyful experiences, I wish the same could happen for all children—that they have many opportunities to experience and enjoy nature, to marvel at birds and climb trees, to scratch at soil and anticipate seasons, to garden, gather pebbles, leap into leaves. We should remember we're all children of nature. Old as we grow, we can still relish breathing in the fresh air, watching clouds roll on, staring into starlight, being astonished by mountains and mystified in moonlight, and awakening every morning to the fiery dawn of life.

I believe this can be one of our best ways to resolve the systemic apathy and inaction suppressing our species: to reacquaint ourselves with nature and, by personal choice, to become students of Earth with an ambition to learn and to graduate into life—not with the diplomas and distinctions of academia but with degrees of deference toward the natural order, which can educate us to live better, more informed, and purposeful lives. Earth is our school, our public university, where we can discover who we really are, what we are here for, what we'd like to be and do when we mature, and how we relate with everything else. Let us attend the many lessons of nature. Let us learn from the earth.

Year 2123

What will Earth look like in one hundred years from 2023? What will be the status of its oceans, its land, its habitats and biodiversity, its natural resources, and its life? How might humans be doing at that point? No, we're *not* forecasting here. We're not imagining, either. Right now, we're viewing 2123 through *you, your* eyes, *your* mind, *your* preference: how *you* would choose to have Earth be at that time.

What do *you* want to see? Will Earth's oceans be rising, flooding coasts and cities? Will drinking water be scarce? Will pollution darken skies? Will species endangered in 2023 have disappeared by 2123? Will Earth be worse off than it is now? Do you envision humanity struggling mightily? Or do you decide something else? Perhaps you would have the opposite: a thriving planet humans preserve mindfully and peacefully.

Remember, though: this is *your wish*, not what you *assume* will happen or expect but rather *what you choose to see.* You see, it all *starts with you.* Issues, and their solutions, begin in thought, which leads to action. If, on the most basic level of consideration, we can generally agree Earth *should* be healthy, we can advance into the future with the comfort of an elementary yet essential consensus.

If we want our world to do well, the reality of 2123 stands a much better chance of being a positive and beautiful time for the planet and for our successors. And it *is* a choice we make. It *is* that easy, that immediate, and that far-reaching: if enough people of all ages and walks of life *do* want to see that better Earth, it only becomes more likely to materialize.

First, though, we need to *allow* for the possibility of a better world. Then we *must want* that possibility, preferring it over all the worse alternatives. If we can manage to reach that simple collective decision—to still have a habitable and healthy Earth in year 2123—humankind has a believable potential to share in and focus upon that universal objective.

Then there can be hope and the necessary harmony for what comes next: the hard work of decades, discussions, debates, new planning and technologies, more studies and data, more accessible knowledge and greater public education. Then humankind can exist as more of a team intent on collaborating and succeeding, and as more of a global community choosing to survive, and ultimately as a family unanimously preferring to protect and preserve its one true home for future generations.

What 2123 will be like is a choice each of us makes *today*.

Anthropocene Thoughts
after NASA Photographs

RE: NASA's "Images of Change"
https://climate.nasa.gov/images-of-change
(main website: https://climate.nasa.gov)

NASA's website "Images of Change" displays two photos side by side: each photo reveals some area where Earth has been altered by things such as temperature variations, natural disasters (e.g. floods or droughts), and intense human activity. This satellite imagery reveals many things, perhaps the simplest of which is that our world is constantly subject to small and large-scale alterations.

These changes, documented through computers orbiting our planet in the form of satellites, are objective and undeniable, not to mention eye-opening and astounding, particularly as we witness natural forces at work along with humankind's ability to transform vast stretches of terrain. NASA's website allows you to drag a vertical slider back and forth over the images to review the "before and after" changes.

NASA lets you explore various examples of such transformations. Here are a few for your consideration:

"Fast   Change   in   Great   Lakes   Ice"
(https://climate.nasa.gov/images-of-
change?id=758#758-fast-change-in-great-lakes-ice)   is
an example of how swiftly (from February 20, 2021 to
March 3, 2021) large areas of land may experience
changes.

Photographs such as "Urban Grown in Las Vegas,
Nevada"   (https://climate.nasa.gov/images-of-
change?id=647#647-urban-growth-in-las-vegas-nevada)
and   "Urban   Expansion   in   Shanghai,   China"
(https://climate.nasa.gov/images-of-
change?id=603#603-urban-expansion-in-shanghai-
china) offer visual indicators of human expansions over
decades.

Similar scenarios exist worldwide. Every day, natural
spaces never once touched by human hands meet with
the sudden upheavals of "human progress." What was
pristine and peaceful becomes polluted and pulverized.
Wherever we go, this sort of activity seems to happen
without end, but there *is* an end. Earth may seem
limitless, but its habitable lands and natural resources
are not inexhaustible. The planet cannot be plundered
perpetually.

We should remember Earth is not apart from our lives,
nor is it something we can do without. Our actions
toward Earth will always result in reactions from Earth:
what we do to it, we do to ourselves, ultimately. The
stronger our actions, the more consequential Earth's

reactions can become. This is why we will want to proceed with heightened mindfulness whenever humans think to level landscapes, vacate forests, displace wildlife, generate waste and pollution, saturate landfills, stress ecosystems, all while consuming resources, which cannot be replenished, at accelerating rates.

It has been suggested we're in the Anthropocene, the proposed first geological epoch defined by humankind's dominance over the planet. It almost sounds inconceivable, yet, when faced with the evidence of NASA's photos, plus data and imagery from other sources like *Google Earth* (earth.google.com) or National Oceanic and Atmospheric Administration's *Climate.gov* website, the photographs speak volumes: humans have reshaped the world and continue to do so at escalating rates our planet cannot sustain endlessly.

With a little logic and common sense, we can review the changes in these photographs and ask basic questions. We can notice the grayness where there was green. We can note where snow and ice have diminished or disappeared. We can see dry land where water once flowed. We can contemplate the cities that were fields once. We can marvel at our human capabilities, our engineering feats, and we can take a good long look at how we, above all other organisms and natural phenomena, have managed to refashion Earth.

Conversing with Gaia

If, as a poet, I suggest nature—Gaia, our mythically maternal Earth—talks to us, you might presume I'm speaking figuratively, using metaphor for effect. I've explored such analogies in my poems, but here I'm going further to say that nature quite *literally* converses with us every single day of our lives.

Of course, Earth has no discernible mouth, no vocal cords, no human means of verbalization. Still, the language of nature resonates deep and wide through patterned physics, symbolic structures, vocabularies of volcanoes and vortices, the wording of winds, the grammar of geology, chemical inflections, the bywords of biology, and more.

These naturally occurring and forthcoming organic orations can be sensed, parsed, read at length, interpreted, and then responded to through our daily actions: that is how we speak with Gaia, whether we realize it or not.

Anyone fluent in the natural world knows nature offers many signs and can respond to human activities in different ways. This "conversation" is not an exclusive act between Earth and us: all nature participates in this lively and candid conference.

Despite their biological differences and singular physiques, plants and animals everywhere heed Gaia's signals and reply by way of physics, biology, and chemistry: secretions, scents, motions, rhythms, music even, and many other ways. It's a dialogue of senses and sensations, chemicals and receptors, microscopic messengers, and elusive energies, all of which trade information below the threshold of human perception.

The most silent forest is full of chatter above and below the ground. Even microscopically, networks of communication form and spread information, be it in brains or nervous systems or further out, in lakes, swamps, or soil under stone.

So far, humans have formally studied some of nature's most elemental expressions—its dialects of DNA, the meanings of its minerals, references embedded in rivers, news of neurons, the lyrical light that sings of life. Fragments of those messages have been transcribed into more humanly understandable terms: mathematical proportions, geometrical patterns, logical operations, structural relationships, rhythms and regularities.

The full range of nature's communication awaits our comprehension and appreciation. Over millions of years, Earth's layered lands and stony shelves amassed extensive libraries of living literature: continuously growing collections of natural histories, biological biographies, existential essays, and perennial poetry, to name a few. All of which could help us learn more about our world, ourselves, and the universe.

Earth will always have important, if not urgent things to tell us, and we cannot ignore our world, collectively or individually, anymore without the risk of missing some point of information which might be central to the survival of all.

If we can afford nature the attention and reverence it deserves and approach it with genuine humility and an eagerness to learn, we may ready ourselves to hear Gaia more clearly, intelligently, and personally. Then we should be prepared to participate more mindfully and meaningfully in the most essential conversations of life.

We Can Be Earthlings

We're all from somewhere. New York. California. Florida. Texas. Canada. South America. France. Spain. Italy. England. Ireland. Africa. India. China. Japan. Somewhere else. We tend to drape ourselves in localities, inclined to describe ourselves as New Yorkers, Californians, and so on, but, as much as we identify with specific locations and cultures, we cannot deny we're also an international family, a global species, planetary citizens, cohabitants of Earth.

We don't have to turn away from who we are, or where we're from, to acknowledge this. Foremost, we should be ourselves, authentic to our respective heritages. We can become aware of our tendency to think regionally. We can also consider how locations might shape our minds and influence our outlooks on the larger world.

We can concede our world is nothing less than the sum of every single place, and that, underneath it all, this planet naturally exists as an *undivided* expanse in all directions from wherever we stand.

From there, perhaps we'll recognize

> this soil we share with the trees,
> with ponds and swamps and flowing streams,

this land that knows we're not confined
by place and time, identities,

or names and claims, economy,
or what we've held and cannot keep.

We're these horizons, oceans, skies,
this wider world of points of view,

a human species, family:
community, not boundaries.

Descendants of the stellar realm, we're members of this
universe, creations flamed with consciousness to probe
unknowns, our purpose here, what we were once and
could become.

We can be Earthlings, global souls,
absolved of walls, old names and lines
scrawled long between ourselves and all.

With eyes as wide horizons go,
and planetary reasoning,
we'll know our boundless fellowship:

our lands of interwoven roots
entangled quantum particles,
and mountains sprouting from one sphere.

Our world unites us, guides us round

the light of sun, toward every star,
the cosmic dawn of who we are:

creation's children, life of lives,
born equal, undivided here,
descendants of unbroken Earth.

Some Earth Words Worth Knowing

Whenever I write something, I prefer it to be accessible—understood and enjoyable by as many readers as possible. More than that, I hope to promote awareness of different topics. With that in mind, I've written this brief glossary of environmental terms.

I'm not much of a fan of technical jargon, but, from my studies over the decades, I also recognize it is important for us to become aware of certain words—at least enough so we can understand and participate in discussions and debates on these kinds of essential topics.

The following definitions are based on my perspectives, experiences, and basic knowledge as a perpetual student of the earth. For more scientific and comprehensive definitions, I encourage you to visit your local library, where you can explore many fine books and reference works about Earth and nature.

~

Acid Rain: Pollution can cause this dangerous kind of rain, which can endanger soil, plants, and organisms.

Anthropocene: A presently *unofficial* but increasingly popular term describing our most recent geological epoch as the first period in Earth's natural history that can be defined by the extraordinary environmental impacts of human activities around the world. Officially, we're said to be in the *Holocene Epoch*, which began around 11,000 years ago.

Atmosphere: Earth is surrounded by gasses, mostly nitrogen and oxygen. That's the atmosphere. There are several layers to the atmosphere. The lowest part, where we're at, is called the *troposphere*. Higher layers (in order, moving upward/outward from the troposphere) are the *stratosphere, mesosphere, thermosphere,* and *exosphere*.

Biome: A large region recognized by its geography, climate, and, most importantly, its unique communities (ecosystems and habitats) of plants (flora) and animals (fauna).

Biodiversity: The biological variety that exists in any given environment. This diversity of life, which develops over many years, can be impacted or destroyed by various forces and factors, such as changing climates, invasive organisms, endangered species, or disruptive or destructive human activities. When biodiversity diminishes or disappears, environments and their organisms may face abnormal changes, imbalance, decline, or eventual devastation due to how interdependent living things in that area have become over many years.

Biosphere: Where all life lives on Earth. The biosphere includes all the environments (*ecosystems* – see definition below) where life exists.

Botany: The scientific study of plants.

Canopy: The living covering provided by the uppermost branches and leaves of trees in a forest as limbs grow close and intermesh. In dense forests and rainforests, canopies can be particularly protective, performing as umbrellas of sorts when it rains hard. Canopies also offer shade from the sun and its heat, resulting in more temperate zones below, which can benefit organisms there.

Carbon: One of the most important substances on Earth. Carbon's unique ability to combine with other elements and to form large, complex, and flexible structures makes life, as we know it on Earth, possible.

Carbon Dioxide: A gas that can have natural as well as industrial origins. For example, we humans inhale oxygen and exhale carbon dioxide, whereas plants can absorb carbon dioxide and release oxygen (a process called **photosynthesis**). When living things pass away, carbon dioxide can be released into the atmosphere. Factories and machinery using "fossil fuels" (such as oil) can release large amounts of carbon dioxide ("carbon emissions"). An overabundance of carbon dioxide contributes to something called the Greenhouse Effect, which causes our planet to grow warmer.

Carbon Footprint: How much carbon dioxide (and other greenhouse gases like methane) someone or something releases back into Earth's environment and atmosphere. The larger the "footprint," the more such emissions are said to be released. Reducing a "carbon footprint" refers to an effort to reduce such emissions, such as consuming less energy, minimizing or eliminating use of "fossil fuels" as energy sources.

Climate: The average temperature, weather, and environmental conditions of a certain area on Earth.

Climate Change: Variations in the otherwise usual weather patterns, temperature ranges, and moisture levels in different areas of the world. The phrases "climate change" and "global warming" are distinct: global warming refers to the measurement of rising temperatures in various regions, whereas climate change encompasses global warming as well as other notable environmental variations.

Climatology: The scientific study of Earth's climate, including its weather patterns, atmospheric phenomena, temperatures, as well as related environmental factors and climatic variations.

Conservation: Minding and managing environmental resources more responsibly and sustainably. The opposite of conservation is the *waste* and *depletion* of natural resources. See also the definition for *sustainability* below.

Cycles: Earth is a place of ceaseless activity and cycles—repetitious natural events that typically go through several stages. There are many kinds of cycles in nature, such as:

- **day and night** – the cycle of sunlight, darkness, and moonlight
- **seasons** – spring, summer, winter, autumn
- **biological cycles**, such as heartbeats, breathing, sleeping and waking, and life cycles (the development, death, and decay of organisms).
- **carbon cycles** - carbon circulating through Earth and its atmosphere due to things like photosynthesis (as plants absorb carbon dioxide and release oxygen) and organisms living, feeding, dying, and decaying in the wild
- **water cycles (hydrologic cycles)** - water moving and transitioning from solid to liquid and to vapor throughout Earth, from bodies of water and land to living things and the atmosphere
- **rock cycles** - the constant formation and erosion of rocks and land
- **ocean tides** that ebb and flow
- **weather, water, and wind motions and patterns**

These cyclical activities serve life and the environment, keeping Earth dynamic and, in certain areas, in a natural state of recycling and renewal. Among other things, these cycles can be seen as Earth's ways of maintaining itself. Any disruption of these natural cycles can harm the environment and devastate habitats and their organisms, including humans.

Desertification: When land turns into a desert.

Earth Science: The scientific study of Earth.

Ecology: The science of environmental and biological relationships—how both organic and inorganic things relate and coexist in any given area. Through ecology, we can explore the living conditions, dependencies, and complexities of these communities (ecosystems), from microscopic life to larger habitats, such as forests.

Ecosystem: Whereas *ecology* is the study of relationships between organisms and their respective environments, *ecosystem* refers to an actual environment, its community of life forms, along with its surrounding environmental factors (such as temperature, weather, geography, soil, habitats, and food sources). Some examples of ecosystems are forests, ponds, streams, and fields. Larger areas, such as an ocean, are considered *biomes* and can contain many ecosystems.

Endangered Species: A group of living things that may be permanently lost if they are not protected from further endangerment. The decline or disappearance of a species can trigger a series of unexpected and detrimental effects which can further endanger an environmental region or another species.

Environmentalism: A belief that the environment, including its organisms and ecosystems, should be kept safe from danger and destruction.

Fauna: Animals.

Flora: Plant life.

Food Chains and **Food Webs:** A food chain describes the usual order of things eaten by one organism after another. One organism might eat something, such as a plant, and a second organism might eat the first organism. For example, a small fish can feed on plankton, and then a medium fish could eat the small fish. Later, a larger fish, such as a shark, might eat the medium fish. A food web describes numerous food chains in any given area. Beyond that, food chains and webs demonstrate how organisms live in a state of interdependency. The disappearance of one or more organisms can disrupt food chains and disturb or destroy an ecosystem.

Fossil: Physical evidence of past organisms that has been preserved. Fossils contribute valuable information to the "fossil record," a history of earlier life forms that paleontologists and other scientists use to learn more about earlier times and organisms from those periods.

Fossil Fuels: A non-renewable energy source derived from organisms that have passed away long ago. Oil and coal are two examples of fossil fuels. When fossil fuels burn, they can give off "greenhouse gases," such as carbon dioxide, which can trap heat in Earths' atmosphere. Unlike "renewable energy sources" like solar energy, fossil fuels get used up and can increase pollution, "greenhouse gases," and acid rain.

Gaia: Inspired by mythology, it is a human-like representation (a "personification") of Earth as a divine maternal being ("Mother Earth"), a source of all life.

Geography: The scientific and expansive study of Earth, including its surface, physical features and environments, human activity, and more.

Geology: The scientific study of Earth's physical composition, from its rocks to its structure and the phenomena contributing to its formation.

Global Warming: A reference to scientific measurements detecting higher than average temperatures in different parts of the world.

Greenhouse Effect: What happens when heat gets trapped by gas and water vapor in Earth's atmosphere. When too much of that happens, Earth becomes warmer, causing climates to vary and ecosystems to be stressed or ruined.

Greenhouse Gas: A gas (like carbon dioxide) that can lead to warmer temperatures on Earth (the "Greenhouse Effect").

Habitat: Where certain organisms usually live under certain environmental conditions. To call something *habitable* is to say it is an area where some kind of life can exist naturally. What's habitable for one organism isn't necessarily so for another: what's good for the goldfish isn't good for the giraffe. This is true of planets as well: Earth is the only known habitable world in our solar system, and there are currently no other known worlds (exoplanets) further out in space that can sustain Earth's life forms.

Hydrosphere: The hydrosphere refers to Earth's water in all its forms and everywhere it exists: streams, rivers, lakes, fog, clouds, rainfall, snow, icebergs, glaciers, oceans, and everywhere else, including underground and in the atmosphere.

Invasive Species: A living thing that enters an environment where it did not occur naturally before. Invasive species have the potential to bring unexpected disruptions or dangerous changes to an environment and any native life there.

Meteorology: The scientific study of Earth's atmosphere and weather patterns.

National Parks: Large areas designated by the U.S. Government as officially protected regions to preserve that land and its wildlife. The U.S. National Park Service maintains the parks and other areas.

Natural Resources: Matter and energy sources found in Earth. Some examples include water, air (oxygen), wood, metal, and natural gas.

Oceanography: The scientific study of Earth's oceans.

Ozone Layer: A protective layer in Earth's atmosphere that blocks harmful energy (UV, or ultraviolet radiation) from the Sun. In the 1980s, scientists discovered and studied what would come to be called the "Ozone Hole," a vast area over Antarctica, where ozone had been depleted due to dangerous chemicals, which were manufactured around the world and used in the past for things like refrigeration and some propellants (CFCs, or chlorofluorocarbons) used previously in spray cans. The "Montreal Protocol," an international treaty went into effect in 1989, helping to slow and reduce ozone depletion, although the Ozone Hole still exists and varies in size from year to year.

Paleontology: The scientific study of past and ancient life. Paleontologists examine the fossilized remains of earlier organisms to learn more about those life forms as well as Earth's natural history.

Pangaea: Many millions of years ago, the Earth was believed to have one big mass of land (a "supercontinent") that eventually broke up into continents which would later form North and South America, Africa, Europe, Asia, Australia, and Antarctica.

Photosynthesis: How organisms (mainly plants) make use of sunlight to derive ("synthesize") nourishment from carbon dioxide and water. This process results in the generation of oxygen and cleaner air.

Renewable Energy: Energy sources not prone to depletion. Solar energy and wind power are two examples.

Renewable Resource: Something that can be used or consumed and then replenished. When used with care and replanted in timely manners, certain plants and trees can function as renewable resources. Some plants can be used for herbs, spices, and pharmaceutical ingredients, while certain trees can contribute heating and building materials. Non-renewable resources include coal and oil: once they're consumed, they're gone.

Sustainability: Sustainability is about the present as much as it is about the future: ensuring current and future generations live in balance with Earth and carefully manage its finite natural resources. Transitioning from non-renewable to renewable energies, engaging in conservation, reducing pollution, recycling materials, creating more biodegradable products, protecting endangered species, and becoming more mindful of ecology and environmental impacts are some of the many ways humans can embrace sustainability and preserve Earth now and for years to come.

Symbiosis: Through ecology, we know that there are many relationships between organisms and their respective environments. Many of these relationships can be described as symbiotic, where organisms derive mutual benefits as they coexist and work together, directly or indirectly. One example is how sharks can be accompanied by smaller fish called remora. Remora attach themselves to sharks and enjoy tiny leftovers from when sharks eat. Remora also help to keep the shark's skin clear of parasites, which, in turn, keeps the shark healthy. Remora also collaborate in the same manner with whales.

Understory: Where living things and vegetation grow near the ground in a forest. The understory, along with the floor of the forest and the underground, helps to establish rich and protective habitats where various organisms and can grow and thrive.

Water Cycle: The more scientific term for this is *hydrologic cycle*. Water cycles through the world in various forms as liquid, snow and ice, and vapor. From organisms to the atmosphere, this cycle circulates water throughout environments, helping to sustain living things and their habitats.

Zoology: The scientific study of animals.

Some Poets of Nature to Explore

If you'd like to read more poems on nature, earth, and ecology, I recommend these poets for your consideration. Of course, many of these poets (Whitman, for example) have written on many topics other than nature. Still, I find their various poetic engagements of the natural world to be notable and worth exploring.

Matsuo Basho
Wendell Berry
Yosa Buson
John Clare
Emily Dickinson
Ralph Waldo Emerson
Robert Frost
Joy Harjo
Robert Hass
Seamus Heaney
Ted Hughes
Issa (Kobayashi Issa)
Robinson Jeffers
Henry Wadsworth Longfellow
Mary Oliver
Masaoka Shiki
Gary Snyder
Alfred Tennyson (Alfred, Lord Tennyson)
Henry David Thoreau
Walt Whitman
William Wordsworth

Nature is one of the oldest and most frequent subjects in the history of poetry. Haiku poets such as Basho and Issa meditated on the natural world throughout their concise but thought-provoking works.

A haiku poem often meditates on natural phenomena, highlighting encounters in nature, such as birds or butterflies, while saying something compelling. Classic haiku includes the *kigo*—words or imagery referring to a season—and that roots such traditional haiku in nature at various times of the year.

Poets from every era and culture drew inspiration from nature. In the Romantic Period, of literature there are poets such as John Clare and William Wordsworth, along with other names worth mentioning, as far as "poets who have written on nature" are concerned: John Keats, Percy Bysshe Shelley, and Samuel Taylor Coleridge.

Gary Snyder, Wendell Berry, Mary Oliver, and Robert Hass all span the 20th and 21st centuries, and offer us many accessible and profound poetic engagements of nature.

If you'd like to read more contemporary "ecopoetry," I suggest the following anthologies:

> *Ecopoetry: A Critical Introduction*
> edited by J. Scott Bryson

The Ecopoetry Anthology
edited by Ann Fisher-Wirth
and Laura-Gray Street,
with an introduction from Robert Hass

Nine Notable Names

There are countless heroes of nature, wildlife, and natural resources. Most of those advocates quietly but passionately carry out their work, raising awareness, protesting on behalf of Earth and living things, promoting sustainability, and more—all without much or any public recognition. Though we will never get to know them all, we should take some moments to thank them for their essential efforts.

Now, as for *known* persons—historic champions of Earth—here are nine notable names everyone should be familiar with:

- **Ansel Adams** – nature photographer and conservationist
- **John James Audubon** –ornithologist, artist, naturalist, author of *The Birds of America*
- **Wendell Berry** – poet and prolific essayist on agriculture, the environment, and sustainability
- **Rachel Carson** – marine biologist, critic of pesticides, author of *Silent Spring* and *The Sea Around Us*
- **Dian Fossey** – zoologist, studied mountain gorillas
- **Jane Goodall** – scientist, conservationist, studied chimpanzees

- **Aldo Leopold** – conservationist, author of *A Sand County Almanac*, helped inspire the Wilderness Act of 1964
- **John Muir** – conservationist, author, helped establish U.S. national parks with Theodore Roosevelt, also help founded Sierra Club
- **Henry David Thoreau** – essayist, author of *Walden*, *Walking*, and more

For longer lists of names, you can visit the following websites:

The National Wildlife Federation: Conservation Hall of Fame
https://www.nwf.org/About-Us/History/Conservation-Hall-of-Fame

Wikipedia articles:

Conservationists
https://en.wikipedia.org/wiki/List_of_conservationists

Ecologists
https://en.wikipedia.org/wiki/List_of_ecologists

Environmentalists
https://en.wikipedia.org/wiki/Environmentalist

As always, please mind Wikipedia's disclaimers:
https://en.wikipedia.org/wiki/Wikipedia:General_disclaimer

lives of plants and trees, their communities and communications, as well as their abilities to react to many different conditions and situations, all *without the luxury of a brain.* It all goes to demonstrate we are indeed part of something larger we do not yet fully comprehend.

This would not be the first time this has happened to humans. The Copernican Revolution helped us move past our ancient and ego-centric Ptolemaic order of the universe, where everything literally revolved around the earthly sphere of humanity. As Copernicus, and others to follow would help us understand, our world connects with something grander, far more complex than we may ever comprehend: the universe. New knowledge gained through science has helped us to revolutionize our thinking, revealing previously unknown truths about our world, and often in mind-blowing manners.

To witness the same revolutionary thinking take root in environmental discussions is also incredible and timely, I think. More and more we are starting to see that Earth is not some cold, impersonal, dead rock that just happens to have a smattering of accidental life on its surface. We're discovering Earth is a more complex system of interdependent and regulatory factors, and our planet has been more environmentally responsive to human activities than we expected.

Where does that leave us in this discussion of empathy? Has science shown Earth is alive? Some would say *yes*.

Fifty Earth Books to Consider

The following list of fifty nonfiction works is far from complete and representative of the finest books ever written on nature. There are far too many excellent books about Earth to list here. These titles are suggested mainly in hopes of offering readers starting points and some opportunities to learn more about nature.

For more reading possibilities, I encourage you to visit your nearest public library, where a librarian could help you to locate books like these, along with even more information on Earth.

Animals, Plants, & Other Living Things

- *Beloved Beasts: Fighting for Life in an Age of Extinction* by Michelle Nijhuis
- *Botany of Desire: A Plant's-Eye View of the World* by Michael Pollan
- *Braiding Sweetgrass: Indigenous Wisdom, Scientific Knowledge and the Teachings of Plants* by Robin Wall Kimmerer
- *Entangled Life: How Fungi Make Our Worlds, Change Our Minds & Shape Our Futures* by Merlin Sheldrake
- *The Hidden Kingdom of Fungi: Exploring the Microscopic World in Our Forests, Homes, and Bodies* by Keith Seifert
- *The Hidden Half of Nature: The Microbial Roots of Life and Health* by David R. Montgomery
- *The Hidden Life of Trees: What They Feel, How They Communicate - Discoveries from a Secret World* by Peter Wohlleben

- *An Immense World: How Animal Senses Reveal the Hidden Realms Around Us* by Ed Yong
- *Jungle: How Tropical Forests Shaped the World and Us* by Patrick Roberts
- *Justice for Animals: Our Collective Responsibility* by Martha C. Nussbaum
- *Living Planet: The Web of Life on Earth* by David Attenborough
- *The Nature of Oaks: The Rich Ecology of Our Most Essential Native Trees* by Douglas W. Tallamy
- *The Rise and Reign of the Mammals: A New History, from the Shadow of the Dinosaurs to Us* by Steve Brusatte
- *The Secret Life of Plants* by Peter Tompkins, Christopher Bird
- *The Secret Wisdom of Nature: Trees, Animals, and the Extraordinary Balance of All Living Things* by Peter Wohlleben
- *The Social Instinct: How Cooperation Shaped the World* by Nichola Raihani
- *The Soul of an Octopus* by Sy Montgomery
- *The Treeline: The Last Forest and the Future of Life on Earth* by Ben Rawlence

Earth

- *A Brief History of Earth: Four Billion Years in Eight Chapters* by Andrew H. Knoll
- *Here on Earth: A Natural History of the Planet* by Tim Flannery
- *Otherlands: A Journey Through Earth's Extinct Worlds* by Thomas Halliday
- *The Story of Earth: The First 4.5 Billion Years, from Stardust to Living Planet* by Robert M. Hazen

- *Timefulness: How Thinking Like a Geologist Can Help Save the World* by Marcia Bjornerud

Ecology, & Environment
- *Abundant Earth: Toward an Ecological Civilization* by Eileen Crist
- *The Anthropocene Reviewed: Essays on a Human-Centered Planet* by John Green
- *The Dream of the Earth* by Thomas Berry
- *Field Notes from a Catastrophe: Man, Nature, and Climate Change* by Elizabeth Kolbert
- *The Future of Life* by Edward O. Wilson
- *The Human Planet: How We Created the Anthropocene* by Simon L. Lewis, Mark A. Maslin
- *Silent Spring* by Rachel Carlson
- *Silent Spring Revolution: John F. Kennedy, Rachel Carson, Lyndon Johnson, Richard Nixon, and the Great Environmental Awakening* by Douglas Brinkley
- *The Sixth Extinction: An Unnatural History* by Elizabeth Kolbert
- *Spiritual Ecology: The Cry of the Earth* edited by Llewellyn Vaughan-Lee
- *The World Without Us* by Alan Weisman

Nature
- *Last Child in the Woods: Saving Our Children from Nature-Deficit Disorder* by Richard Louv
- *The Nature of Nature: Why We Need the Wild* by Enric Sala
- *Nature's Best Hope: A New Approach to Conservation That Starts in Your Yard* by Douglas W. Tallamy

- *The Nature Principle: Reconnecting with Life in a Virtual Age* by Richard Louv
- *Pilgrim at Tinker Creek* by Annie Dillard
- *The Sacred Balance: Rediscovering Our Place in Nature* by David Suzuki
- *Sacred Nature: Restoring Our Ancient Bond with the Natural World* by Karen Armstrong
- *The Sense of Wonder: A Celebration of Nature for Parents and Children* by Rachel Carlson
- *Upstream: Selected Essays* by Mary Oliver
- *Walden* by Henry David Thoreau

Water & Bodies of Water

- *The Death and Life of the Great Lakes* by Dan Egan
- *Rivers of Power: How a Natural Force Raised Kingdoms, Destroyed Civilizations, and Shapes Our World* by Laurence C. Smith
- *The Sea Around Us* by Rachel Carson
- *Still Waters: The Secret World of Lakes* by Curt Stager
- *The Water Will Come: Rising Seas, Sinking Cities, and the Remaking of the Civilized World* by Jeff Goodell
- *Where the Water Goes: Life and Death Along the Colorado River* by David Owen

Websites for Further Exploration

There are many excellent websites which can help you learn more about Earth, ecology, and many other environmental concepts and issues. Here are a few websites for your consideration:

From **NASA** (National Aeronautics and Space Administration):

> **Earth Observatory**
> earthobservatory.nasa.gov
>
> **Explore Earth**
> www.nasa.gov/topics/earth
>
> **Global Climate Change**
> climate.nasa.gov

National Audubon Society
www.Audubon.org

National Geographic
www.NationalGeographic.com

National Park Service
www.nps.gov

National Wildlife Federation
www.nwf.org

Smithsonian: Science & Conservation
www.si.edu/explore/science

U.S. Environmental Protection Agency (EPA)
www.EPA.gov

U.S. Fish and Wildlife Service (FWS)
www.FWS.gov

U.S. Forest Service, USDA (U.S. Dept. of Agriculture)
www.fs.usda.gov

U.S. Geological Survey (USGS)
www.USGS.gov

U.S. National Oceanic and Atmospheric Administration (NOAA)
www.NOAA.gov (see also www.Climate.gov)

U.S. National Park Service (NPS)
www.NPS.gov

UN Environment Programme
www.UNEP.org

See also the UN's **Intergovernmental Panel on Climate Change** (IPCC)
www.ipcc.ch

Crafting a Creed for Earth

From a distance, environmentalist, conservationist, green, and other ecological movements may seem alike, but each of them approaches environmental concerns with different aims and proposed solutions.

Despite those varied viewpoints, I've wondered if a kind of universal creed is possible—perhaps at least a basic set of principles nature lovers and environmental defenders might recognize and rally around while advocating Earth's conservation and protection.

Here's my *very* basic attempt at a first draft of such a theoretical statement:

Earth Credo

Earth is our home, our habitat,
a vital realm we should conserve.

We champion balance, peace, and care
so life abides and Earth might thrive.

May human products, ways, and deeds
cause no harm for the world or sky.

Earth's resources must not be drained.
May we consume things mindfully.

May we renew where we deplete,
restore what's damaged or destroyed.

May we embrace diversity,
endorse sustainability,

seek justice and equality
for nature, us, and everyone.

May we proceed with empathy,
full consciousness of future life,

the generations to arrive,
and leave no worse a world for them.

May science guide us to become
fit residents deserving Earth.

Earth Empathy

The very suggestion of *empathizing with Earth* might seem absurd. You might question my use of the word *empathy*, since it implies *Earth has feelings*, and perhaps you wonder if I meant to say *sympathy*. You might disapprove of the notion and point out Earth has no emotional capacity, and that it's neither alive nor conscious or able to communicate. You might also advise against attributing any human (*anthropomorphic*) qualities to our planet. And many people would agree with you.

Conceiving of a planet that's animate and sensitive can be perplexing or unnerving. It wasn't long ago that humans were hesitant to suggest animals possessed any degree of intelligence, complex speech, or emotional capacity. Zoologists and others have shown us otherwise. Dolphins, elephants, chimpanzees, whales, and other creatures mourn their dead in very visible and unmistakable ways. The octopus, gorilla, and crow are just a few examples of animals exhibiting reasoning and problem-solving abilities.

We've underestimated nature time and again, presuming humans are the sole proprietors of intellect and feelings, but that sort of thinking is starting to change. A growing number of books by authors like Peter Wohlleben now promote awareness about the

Others will still dissent. To this day, disagreements persist as to what constitutes life. It's an ever-debated subject with implications that go well beyond science. Meanwhile, our planet experiences the brunt of human industry and vanity every single day—activities which can cause environmental disruption and destruction.

So, while we could sit here, exchanging lofty opinions on the matter of Earth's aliveness, weighing and arguing to no particular end, there are very real consequences arising from human inconsideration toward Earth. Rather than wait for scientific researchers to achieve a consensus and produce a definitive statement conceding *Earth is alive* in some abstract sense, let us entertain this concept seriously, at least within the scope of this essay.

Of course, it's an assertion that would attract resistance, derision, and dismissal. In the 1970s, two scientists, James Lovelock and Lynn Margulis, collaborated on what is known as the Gaia Hypothesis, which considered Earth's organic complexity and abilities to self-regulate. Aspects of that theory would mature and find acceptance in the field of *earth system science*, but new debates and ideas continue to emerge.

I have an easy solution to this: *metaphor*, the poet's most powerful way of paralleling and comparing seemingly dissimilar things by simply saying *A is B*. So, we're going to think *metaphorically* instead here. We're outright saying *Earth is a person*. What kind of person?

A friend, perhaps, or a neighbor, or a mother. Someone. And now we can start to consider how this person has managed, being at the receiving end of human activities for so long.

Stepping into that someone's shoes, how would we feel, given what we know about humans and the environment? Let us, for a little while, observe life, history, and humanity through Earth's perspective. What could we see? How might we feel? What would we want? These can be very helpful and revealing inquiries, I believe, because they have the potential of compelling contemplation as we regard the sorrows of our battered world and attempt to answer these questions.

Let us step forth and put ourselves in our planet's place. And let us invoke the Golden Rule, treating our world as we wish to be treated. If we see humans are a part of nature, just as Earth is, it is not preposterous to suggest Earth deserves kindness and compassion, because we believe we are entitled to these very things. We risk being foolish, reckless, or even cruel if we were to suggest otherwise.

We *should* share in every pain and setback we cause our planet, just as much as we would want to share in the hope and the joy and the love we cultivate when we care for the environment. Nature *is* reciprocal, cyclical, symbiotic, entangled by interdependent things. If we really want better things to come of our deeds, benevolence and diligence will be essential to our cause, as will humility and patience.

Everything we introduce into the natural order of life eventually comes full circle. Once we understand that, we can more clearly appreciate the immediacy and consequences of our most casual or careless decisions. May we choose to live more considerately and to encourage humanity to foster and express the very goodwill and cooperation it anticipates in kind from nature. May Earth receive the fullness of human empathy, and may we meet much goodness in return.

About the Author

Robert J. Tiess is a poet, musician, artist, and nature lover from New York State, where he has lived all his life.

A graduate of SUNY New Paltz University with a degree in English Literature, Robert has been writing poetry since the 1980s and pursuing a joyful career in public library service since the mid-1990s.

In September 2022, Robert married the love of his life, Sandra.

You can learn more about the author and his poetry in his debut poetry collection (2022), *The Humbling and Other Poems*.

For Robert's website, social media links, and more, please visit **www.RobertJTiess.net**

Also by the Author

The Humbling and Other Poems

Robert's debut poetry collection, which was featured as an "Editor's Pick" in the June 20, 2022 issue of *Publishers Weekly*, features over 100 poems on humility, love, truth, peace, redemption, and hope.

Bonus materials in the book include a glossary of poetry terms, reading suggestions, three brief essays, and more.

The Humbling and Other Poems is available in a variety of print and digital eBook formats.

Please visit **www.RobertJTiess.net** for more information, reviews, and websites.

www.ingramcontent.com/pod-product-compliance
Lightning Source LLC
Chambersburg PA
CBHW032103280326